THE LOUISVILLE SLUGGER

BOOK OF
GREAT HITTERS

D. W. Crisfield

A MOUNTAIN LION BOOK

John Wiley & Sons, Inc.
New York • Chichester • Weinheim • Brisbane • Singapore • Toronto

ISBN 0-471-19772-6

Printed in the United States of America
10 9 8 7 6 5 4 3 2 1

Dedication

I'd like to thank Linda O'Malley, for her research efforts on my behalf; Carrie Wickenden, for her messenger work; Jennifer Feltes, for taking the kids; Doug Myers, for his fountain of knowledge; Bill Melchior, the public relations man in the American League office; Glenn Wilburn, public relations man in the National League office; and JAC, JDC, CBC, who put up with a lot.

—*D.W. Crisfield*

Acknowledgments

This book was conceived, developed, and produced by Mountain Lion, Inc., a book producer that specializes in instructional and general reference books in the sports category. A book producer brings together and relies on the special skills of many people. The following people contributed to producing *The Louisville Slugger Book of Great Hitters* and to all of them we say, "Thanks."

Debbie Crisfield, author; John Monteleone, president of Mountain Lion; Kate Bradford, editor of the Professional and Trade Division at John Wiley & Sons; Mark Gola, managing editor at Mountain Lion; Randy Voorhees, sales and marketing director at Mountain Lion; Margaret Trejo, Trejo Production, composition; Max Crandall, designer; Alicia Bryzycki, copyeditor and proofreader; Deborah Patton, indexer; and Joan Mohan, office manager at Mountain Lion.

Also: Michael Plunkett, photographer; Andy Anderson, curator, photography archives, Ekstrom Library, University of Louisville; Ellen Pollack, photo researcher; Joanna Bruno, sales representative, AP Wide World Photos; and Marci Harrington, photo department representative at the National Baseball Hall of Fame Museum, Inc.

Contents

Introduction

Hitters, hitters, and more hitters. That's what readers of *The Louisville Slugger Book of Great Hitters* will find on every page. From Hank Aaron to Robin Yount, the feats of 100 of baseball's all-time greatest hitters are revealed through amazing stories, action photographs, and lifetime statistics and records. It's all here: the great performers, the magic moments, all-time hitting records, and lots of cool trivia.

The Louisville Slugger name is well known to baseball fans of every age. The folks in Louisville have been making bats for baseball players for over 100 years; from the tiniest Little Leaguer to the great Babe Ruth, generation after generation of hitters have used Louisville Slugger bats to torment pitchers and set records.

This book was as much fun to write as it is to read. Researching players from the past and present taught me a lot about how much the game has changed. But, remarkably, it taught me even more about how much in baseball has not changed; particularly when it comes to hitting records. For example, Joe DiMaggio's record 56-game hitting streak, set in 1941, has not been seriously challenged since. That same year Ted Williams became the last player to bat over .400 for a season (.406). So despite Astroturf fields, livelier baseballs, and smaller stadiums, our modern sluggers still have records to shoot for that are older than they are.

You'll read about unusual characters such as Wade Boggs, who is so superstitious that he will only eat chicken before a game. You'll read about unusual records, such as Ken Griffey Jr. and his dad, Ken Griffey Sr., who became the only father and son to hit home runs in the same game.

The book features some of the truly great baseball nicknames, too. There's "the Say Hey Kid" (Willie Mays), "the Georgia Peach" (Ty Cobb), "the Sultan of Swat" (Babe Ruth), "the Crime Dog" (Fred McGriff), and "the Big Hurt" (Frank Thomas). It seems that men who are good with a bat in their hands get the best nicknames.

My goal in writing *The Louisville Slugger Book of Great Hitters* was to create a celebration of those men who were, and are, the very best at hitting a baseball. And maybe, just maybe, some kids who read this book will be inspired to become the hitting legends of tomorrow. Batter up!

D. W. Crisfield
October 1997

Hank Aaron

Henry Louis "Hammerin' Hank" Aaron is the all-time home run leader in baseball, having crushed 755 of them. He hit over 20 home runs in a season for 20 years in a row. Eight times he reached the 40 mark or higher. He is also the all-time RBI leader, with 2,297. He's third in hits, with 3,771. His lifetime average was .305. He was inducted into the Hall of Fame in 1982.

A Block of Strength

Hank Aaron was born on February 5, 1934, in Mobile, Alabama, one of eight children. As a boy, he liked to hit bottle caps with a broomstick. He helped out his family by earning money by delivering ice in the neighborhood. Looking back, Henry believed that lifting the 25-pound blocks of ice helped him develop his strong, quick wrists. His high school didn't have a baseball team, so Hank first played softball and then moved on to the Negro Leagues.

Signed by the Indianapolis Clowns, Aaron began playing semipro ball at age 16. A young player who had never been taught any of the fundamentals of hitting, Aaron took his swing with a cross-handed grip. A scout advised him to switch to a regular grip, and he responded by hitting two home runs in his first game.

The Milwaukee Braves bought Aaron's contract in 1952 and sent him to play in the minor leagues. He hit .336 in his first season and led the league with a .362 average the following season.

In 1954 he got his big break with the Braves. One of the outfielders had broken his ankle. There was room for Hank. He moved up from the minors and hit .280, with 13 home runs and 69 RBIs. Then he broke his own ankle. He came back even stronger the next season, though, and hit .314 with 27 homers and 106 RBIs. The Braves had found a slugger.

Hank Aaron wasn't nervous at the plate. The way he saw it, he had an advantage. "The pitcher has got only a ball. I've got a bat. So the percentage in weapons is in my favor, and I let the fellow with the ball do the fretting."

Aaron went on to some remarkable achievements. He hit over 20 home runs for 20 years in a row, leading the league four times. He captured the batting crown twice and the slugging crown four times. He led several times each in hits, runs, doubles, and RBIs. He won the Most Valuable Player (MVP) award only once, however, in 1957. That year he hit .322, with 44 home runs and 132 RBIs. In the World Series he hit .393, with three home runs to help the Braves win the championship in seven games.

Though he hit home run after home run throughout his career, Aaron was not a very big guy. He didn't have bulging biceps like José Canseco or the intimidating stature of Mark McGwire. Aaron had extremely quick and powerful wrists. He generated his power with tremendous bat speed, hitting homers to all parts of the park.

Twice a First

In 1970 an infield single in Cincinnati gave him his 3,000th hit. It was the first time a black player had become a member of that club, and it was the first time any player had ever achieved the goal while also hitting 500 home runs. After Aaron had crossed home plate, Stan Musial, the only other living member of the club, jumped over the fence to congratulate him. "It was getting awfully lonely," he said.

That milestone felt good. The next one, Babe Ruth's all-time home run record, was getting harder to enjoy. As Hank approached the magic number 714, fans started to object. It seems that half the country was excited that the record might be broken, and the other half thought it was the worst thing that could happen to baseball. When Roger Maris broke Babe Ruth's single season record 12 years earlier he, too, was

criticized. He was stepping on the toes of an icon. Think about it. No one is going to step forward to protest if someone is going to beat Maris's record or even Hank Aaron's record. But knocking the Babe off the top was something else altogether.

The Ghost of Ruth

Aaron had it even worse. With Maris, the naysayers could downplay the achievement. Maris's record could have an asterisk by it because Ruth played a shorter season. Hank Aaron's moment in the sun was an out-and-out breaking of the game's most impressive record. Secondly, Aaron was black, and he kept to himself. Ruth was white and a friendly, beloved hero. Many people believed that Aaron did not have the right to break the record because his personality was all wrong for the role. He never even smiled after he hit a home run. Aaron himself recognized the difference between him and Ruth. He assured the public that no one could replace the Babe. He said, "I'm not trying to break any record of Babe Ruth. I'm just trying to make one of my own."

It didn't help. Hank Aaron received death threats and hate mail. His children and even his parents were threatened. The FBI was brought in to investigate some of the more dangerous sounding threats and Hank Aaron was given a police escort for a while. Fortunately, nothing ever came of it, but it did take some of the glow away from the record.

A Short Swing into History

There was thought that he might break it by the end of the 1973 season. But that season ended with Aaron's season total at 40 and his lifetime total at 713. It was about as bad as it could be. Aaron had to endure an entire winter of pressure.

The media attention was relentless in the off-season, but even worse were the death threats. Aaron sometimes wondered if he would make it to opening day. Fortunately, the racists who hassled him were nothing but ignorant cowards. No actual attempts to harm Aaron ever came to pass.

itchers eventually learned that it was a risk to throw fastballs to Hank Aaron. Pitcher Curt Simmons once said, "Throwing a fastball by Henry Aaron is like trying to sneak sunrise past a rooster." The pitchers knew it, and Aaron knew it, too. "I never worried about the fastball. They couldn't throw it past me. None of them."

On opening day Aaron tied the record with his first swing of the season. Shortly thereafter, on April 8, 1974, Hank Aaron slugged number 715 right into the bullpen. He took off around the bases with the crowd wildly cheering, and this time there was a smile on his face. They stopped the game when he reached home plate. "Thank God it's over," was Hank Aaron's reaction.

But actually it wasn't quite over. Aaron went on to hit 40 more home runs over the next three seasons. When he retired in 1976, he could claim 755. He was inducted into the Hall of Fame in 1982, the last player from the Negro League to play in the majors.

CAREER STATISTICS

Batting average	.305
At bats	12,364
Hits	3,771
Doubles	624
Triples	98
Home runs	755
Runs scored	2,174
Runs batted in	2,297
Walks	1,402

Cap Anson

*C*ap "Pops" Anson was the first player to get 3,000 hits. He batted over .300 in all but three of his 22 National League (NL) seasons; twice he hit over .400. He came up with the hit-and-run play and a number of other still popular strategies. He was inducted into the Hall of Fame in 1939.

The Best Player of the Nineteenth Century

If baseball had ended before the 1900s ever started, Adrian "Cap" Anson would have been considered the sport's greatest player. During his 22-year reign as a Chicago White Stocking first baseman and manager, he made his mark on the leader board nearly every year. He led in RBIs nine times, batting average two times, slugging percentage three times, and one year each for walks and stolen bases.

Although Cap Anson will always be remembered as a Chicago player, he did play for two other teams first. In 1870 he dropped out of Notre Dame to join the Rockford Forest Citys, and a year later he was playing for the Philadelphia Athletics. It was when the National League (NL) was formed in 1876 that he joined the Chicago White Stockings.

Unfortunately, Cap Anson's personality will also go down in the history books. He had a foul mouth and a bad temper and is given most of the blame for baseball's 62-year ban on black players. He threatened to organize a strike if they were allowed to play, so black players were "unofficially" banned.

CAREER STATISTICS

Batting average	.329
At bats	9,108
Hits	3,000
Doubles	528
Triples	124
Home runs	96
Runs scored	1,719
Runs Batted In	1,715
Walks	952

Jeff Bagwell

Jeffrey Robert Bagwell is the first baseman for the Houston Astros. He has a career batting average of .304. He's had double-digit home runs in every year of his major league career, and he's led the league in doubles twice.

Hot, but Hurt

In 1995 Jeff Bagwell was on a hot streak. During the month of July alone he batted .330, with seven homers and 31 RBIs. The 31 runs he knocked in before July 30 were the highest monthly total in Astro history, and he even had two more days left in the month. Jeff Bagwell was on fire. But it was not to be. On July 30, in his second plate appearance, Jeff was hit in the left hand by a pitch. The pitch broke a bone. It was the third time in three years he went on the disabled list.

Jeff returned to the lineup with a new piece of batting equipment. He had a specially designed batting glove to protect his hand. It used the same technology as football pads. It had a plastic plate and air cushions. If he ever got hit again, he would be safe.

The glove must have inspired confidence in him because he came back getting a hit in ten out of his first 11 games. He ended the year with a .315 average, 31 home runs, a league-leading 48 doubles, and 120 RBIs. Not bad for a man with a broken hand.

Give Him a Hand

Jeff Bagwell is used to the broken hand routine. He lost the end of the 1993 season as well as the end of the 1994 season to broken hands, but in between he had his MVP year. It was the strike-shortened year, but Bagwell still put up incredible numbers.

His average was .368. He led the league with 104 runs and 116 RBIs. He clubbed 39 homers and 32 doubles. With those stats, he became the first major leaguer since Carl Yastrzemski in 1967 to finish either first or second in all the major hitting categories. He was the first National Leaguer to do it since Willie Mays did it in 1955.

Joining the Big Boys

That year Bagwell was voted the NL MVP in a unanimous vote. It was only the eleventh time in history that the vote had been unanimous. (Oddly enough, it was unanimous the year before with Frank Thomas.) It also made him one of three players to earn the NL MVP award and Rookie of the Year award within four years of each other. Jackie Robinson and Johnny Bench did it within three.

You can always tell when Jeff Bagwell is up at the plate because of his unique batting stance. His legs are very far apart, and he crouches down as if he were sitting on a chair. Strong legs and a muscular upper body give Bagwell the power he needs to hit plenty of balls out of the park.

Now that Jeff Bagwell has his special glove, he can go about breaking records rather than bones. The Houston Astros changed the dimensions of their park, moving the walls in order to make it more hitter-friendly. Jeff Bagwell hardly needs the help—his homers go sailing way past the old mark.

On May 29, 1996 Jeff Bagwell homered twice at Three Rivers Stadium in Pittsburgh. His first home run of that day went into the upper deck. Five years earlier he had done the same thing. Only ten homers have ever reached that height at Three Rivers. Willie Stargell hit four of them and, with his second, Jeff joined him as the only other player to hit more than one into the upper deck.

CAREER STATISTICS

Batting average	.304
At bats	3,457
Hits	1,112
Doubles	246
Triples	20
Home runs	187
Runs scored	654
Runs batted in	724
Walks	627

Home Run Baker

John Franklin "Home Run" Baker was one of the top sluggers of his time. He was a third baseman for the Philadelphia Athletics and the New York Yankees and was always at the top of the league in doubles, triples, and, of course, home runs. His career batting average was .307, and he led the league in home runs from 1911 through 1914.

With a nickname like "Home Run," Frank Baker should have had numbers like Hank Aaron or Babe Ruth. Not even close. Although he did lead the league in home runs for four years straight from 1911 through 1914, he totalled only 96 in his career.

World Series Hero

He earned his nickname, however, from a specific incident. In the second game of the 1911 World Series, he hit a home run off of Rube Marquard to win the game for Philadelphia. Marquard's teammate, Christy Mathewson, let it be known that he thought the home run was a result of Marquard's careless pitching. He had to eat his words, though, the next day, when Baker homered off him in the ninth to tie the game. Philadelphia went on to win, and Frank Baker was known as Home Run Baker from that moment on.

CAREER STATISTICS

Batting average	.307
At bats	5,985
Hits	1,838
Doubles	313
Triples	103
Home runs	96
Runs scored	887
Runs batted in	1,013
Walks	473

Ernie Banks

Ernest "Mr. Cub" Banks hit 512 career home runs, tying him with Eddie Mathews for the number 12 spot on the all-time list. He hit 40 or more in a season five times. He was the first NL player to be elected MVP two years in a row. Banks was inducted into the Hall of Fame in 1977.

Ernie Banks was born in 1931 in Dallas, Texas. He was a four-sport athlete in high school, excelling in everything. He started in the Negro Leagues after graduation from high school, but had to leave after a year when he was drafted into the army. When he got out, he went back to baseball and back to the Negro Leagues. He played his cards right, with some help from his manager, and wouldn't sign with a minor league club. He was going straight to the majors. The Cubs took the gamble, and it paid off.

Money in the Bank

In his first full season he put up decent numbers, but then his hitting exploded. For five of the next six years, he hit over 40 home runs, leading the league twice. In 1955 he hit a record-setting five grand slams. In 1958 and 1959 he also topped the charts in RBIs and turned in a batting average over .300. He won the MVP award for both of those years, becoming the first NL player to win back-to-back. He also was the first MVP on a losing team. In Ernie Banks's 19 years with the team, the Cubs never even won a pennant, much less the World Series.

Slim but Strong

Although he was known as a power hitter, Banks did not have the beefy look of a lot of sluggers. He was 6'1" and about 180 pounds.

But he did have muscle. And he was known as a "wrist hitter," which meant that most of his power was generated by the quick snap of his incredibly strong wrists.

He began his Cub career as the team's shortstop, and he did well there. But in 1961, he hurt his knee and no longer had the agility to play there. Since his hitting didn't seem to be affected, the Cubs just moved him to first base, where he played for the last ten years of his career.

Let's Play Two

Even though he had to overcome racial biases, being the Cubs first black player, he quickly became a fan favorite. They called him "Mr. Cub" and turned out in droves to watch him play. His love for the game was clear to everyone. The Cubs needed enthusiasm like that since they lost a lot of games.

Ernie Banks holds two slugging records for shortstops in a season. In 1958 he clubbed 47 home runs. The following season, Banks drove in an incredible 143 runs. Both records still stand today.

Banks was the player who is responsible for the now-famous saying, "Nice day for baseball. Let's play two." Even when Banks retired in 1971, they kept him in the organization. He stayed in Chicago, working for the Cubs behind the scenes. The franchise couldn't do enough for him, but they did give him the team's top honor. Ernie Banks was the first Cub to have his uniform retired.

CAREER STATISTICS

Batting average	.274
At bats	9,421
Hits	2,583
Doubles	407
Triples	90
Home runs	512
Runs scored	1,305
Runs batted in	1,636
Walks	763

Cool Papa Bell

James Thomas "Cool Papa" Bell
played professional baseball for
an amazing 29 years. His career
batting average was .337; in
exhibition games against major
leaguers, it was .395. He was
inducted into the Hall of Fame in
1974.

Cool Papa Bell has no major league
numbers because he was never
allowed to play for the major
leagues. Even though Jackie
Robinson broke the color barrier
during the last three years of Bell's
career, Cool Papa Bell began and
ended his career in the Negro
Leagues. But his Negro Leagues
numbers speak volumes. He played
for 29 years, yet he still managed to
have a career batting average of .337.

Lightning Speed

Cool Papa was a switch hitter, with incredible
speed on the bases. Some people think he
was the fastest player ever to play professional baseball. Many of his hits came from
bunts or routine infield grounders that he
beat out. But the infield couldn't play in to
catch him. He was a threat to hit home runs,
especially when he was batting right-handed.
Many ballparks during his time had no
outfield fences, so balls could roll a great
distance. He once hit three inside-the-park
home runs in a single game.

Although Bell's statistics are reasonably
accurate, they are incomplete. The Negro
Leagues didn't always keep records. Bell
remembers one game: "I got five hits and
stole five bases, but none of that was written
down because they didn't bring the scorebook
to the game that day."

CAREER STATISTICS	
Batting average	.337
At bats	3,687
Hits	1,241
Doubles	194
Triples	64
Home runs	63
Runs scored	N/A
Runs batted in	N/A
Walks	N/A

N/A = Complete statistics are not available.

Albert Belle

Albert Jojuan Belle is Chicago White Sox left fielder. He is a Babe Ruth slugger with a Ty Cobb personality. He hit 50 home runs in 1995 and 48 in 1996. With 103 extra base hits in 1995, he's fourth on the all-time single-season list, tied with Chuck Klein, Stan Musial, and Hank Greenberg.

Albert Belle grew up in Shreveport, Louisiana, and was known as Joey to his friends and family. Since he was a youngster, he always wanted to win and he's always been a perfectionist. He graduated sixth in his class in high school and was one of the school's top athletes.

Short Fuse on the Field

He went on the Louisiana State University to play college baseball, and there his temper started to get the better of him. He threw bats, helmets, and anything he could get his hands on. But he still knew how to hit. Everyone knew he was a shoe-in for the first round of the draft. At least he was until his coach benched him during the College World Series for one of his temper tantrums. The pro teams got nervous. They figured if the coach could bench a player that good during the College World Series, then he must have some discipline problems. None of the teams picked him until the second round, which Belle figures cost him at least $40,000.

There's no need to worry about money now. The Chicago White Sox are paying Belle $11 million to perform his magic at the plate. And magic it is. In 1991, his first full season, Belle hit .282, belted 28 home runs, and drove in 95 runs. And he just got better from there. In 1992 he hit 34 home runs. In 1993 he hit 38 and led the league in RBIs with 129. In 1994 he hit a mere 36 because of the strike-shortened season but managed to compile a batting average of .357 at the same time.

An Explosive Performance

And then came the 1995 and 1996 seasons. In 1995 Albert Belle hit .317, belted 50 home runs, smacked 52 doubles, and knocked in 126 RBIs. He led the league in homers, doubles, RBIs, and runs. The next year the world was watching to see if he could be the first player since Babe Ruth to have back-to-back seasons of 50 home runs or more. Belle was two dingers short, but his 148 RBIs led the league and were the most by any player since Ted Williams.

After being suspended for corking his bat in 1994, Albert Belle returned to hit .476, with ten home runs in the final 20 games of the season.

Despite his spectacular year, Belle was runner-up for the MVP award in the American League (AL). Many people blame it on the fact that he alienated the sports writers, the ones who vote for the award. It's not out of the question.

Belle's tantrums are famous. He threw a baseball at one photographer, leaving him with a bloodied hand. He screamed and cursed at a reporter in the locker room and was fined $50,000. He chased trick or treaters with his car, threatening to kill them, after they egged his house. He pulled a sink off the wall of the clubhouse and smashed it with his bat. He was suspended in 1994 for using a corked bat. And he was sent to the minors for refusing to run out ground balls.

Not a Bad Guy

Despite all his incidents, Belle remained a popular guy in Cleveland. The Indians' general manager John Hart has said, "95 to 98 percent of the times Albert's a delight to be around." His teammates agree. The Cleveland fans loved him, too, until he rejected the offer the Indians made, which would have made him the highest-paid player in baseball. Instead he signed with the higher-paying White Sox.

It remains to be seen how Albert Belle will be remembered. As the Cleveland general manager Hart says, "He's going to have one of the most prolific offensive careers in history." Let's hope that will be his legacy.

CAREER STATISTICS

Batting average	.291
At bats	4,075
Hits	1,188
Doubles	268
Triples	17
Home runs	272
Runs scored	682
Runs batted in	867
Walks	449

Johnny Bench

Johnny Lee Bench is considered one of the top catchers in the history of baseball. When he retired he had set the record for most home runs by a catcher with 327 (plus 62 at other positions). He led the league twice in home runs and three times in RBIs, and he was inducted into the Hall of Fame in 1989.

Born to Be a Bomber

Johnny Bench was born on December 7, 1947, five years to the day after the sneak attack on Pearl Harbor (this might explain the ease with which he hit the long bomb, but there was certainly never anything sneaky about Johnny Bench's attack). Johnny Bench was known for being a clutch hitter and a power hitter.

Johnny Bench, like Joe Morgan, was another cog in "the Big Red Machine." He earned Rookie of the Year honors in his first full year with them, with a .275 average, 15 home runs, and 82 RBIs. He spent his entire career with Cincinnati, helping them to six division championships and four World Series. In 11 out of 12 seasons, he hit over 20 home runs. And in 1970 and 1972, he clubbed over 40 of them to capture the league titles. Those years he also captured the MVP award and, not surprisingly, those were two years that Cincinnati ended up in the World Series.

CAREER STATISTICS	
Batting average	.267
At bats	7,658
Hits	2,048
Doubles	381
Triples	24
Home runs	389
Runs scored	1,091
Runs batted in	1,376
Walks	891

Yogi Berra

Lawrence Peter "Yogi" Berra was one of baseball's great personalities as well as one of the game's great hitters. He played all but four games of his career for the New York Yankees and went to the World Series 14 times. It was there that he racked up his Hall of Fame numbers. He was inducted in 1972.

Yogi Berra was born in a tough St. Louis neighborhood in 1925. He was solidly built and didn't look much like a baseball player, but he knew how to hit. When he joined the Yankees in 1946, hitting was his only strong point. But they brought in Bill Dickey to coach him on how to catch. He was a quick learner and soon he was great at that, too.

Big Numbers in October

Yogi Berra had ten seasons where he hit over 20 home runs. He had five seasons where he knocked in over 100 RBIs. And he was voted the league's MVP three times in his career, without ever leading the league in a single category. But his World Series numbers are the most impressive. Berra played in more World Series games than any other player, appearing in 75 of them. In World Series statistics, he is first in at bats (259), first in hits (71), first in doubles (10), third in home runs (12), second in runs (41) and RBIs (39), and third in walks (32).

It's not surprising that Yogi performed well in the World Series. He was known for being good in the clutch. Even though he frequently swung at pitches out of the strike zone, he rarely struck out.

CAREER STATISTICS

Batting average	.285
At bats	7,555
Hits	2,150
Doubles	321
Triples	49
Home runs	358
Runs scored	1,175
Runs batted in	1,430
Walks	704

Wade Boggs

Wade Anthony Boggs is the New York Yankees third baseman and one of the game's current top average hitters. He had 200+ hits in seven straight seasons, a major league record. He's hit over .300 for all but two of his 16 years. His lifetime average so far is .331, and he's been elected to the All Star game 11 times.

Wade Boggs played shortstop for his high school team in Florida and was the team's MVP. He was also All-Conference, All-State, and All-American. Those honors earned him the attention of the Boston Red Sox. They signed him in the seventh round of the draft in 1976. He played in the minors for six years. After he led the Triple-A league in average, hits, and doubles and hit over .300 for the fifth year in a row, the Red Sox finally decided it was time to bring him up.

Rookie Sensation

In his first year with the Red Sox, Boggs hit .349, setting the AL rookie record. He lost out on the Rookie of the Year award, coming in third behind Cal Ripken and Kent Hrbek, both of whom had lower averages but slugged more than 20 home runs. He also lost out on the batting title because the Red Sox had only played him in 104 games that year. He'd been called up when Carney Lansford injured his ankle and then was benched, despite his league-leading average when Lansford came back.

Boggs had a full-time job the next year, though, and he won the batting title with an average of .361. He had 210 hits that year and continued to get over 200 hits a season for seven straight years. This set a modern-era major league record for most consecutive seasons, with over 200 hits. The all-time record goes to Willie Keeler, who had eight before the turn of the century.

Boggs also hit over .325 for eight years straight, and in four of those seasons he hit over .360. He won the batting crown five times. He's tied for third on the all-time list for consecutive .300 seasons from the start of a career.

Good Stick, Great Eye

His biggest claim to fame, however, comes when his walks and hits are combined. He's become one of only ten players to get 200 hits and 100 walks in the same season. Lou Gehrig did it for seven seasons. Boggs comes in second with four seasons, beating Babe Ruth with three, Stan Musial with two, and six others with one each.

In the 1987 season, Boggs hit 24 home runs to go with his .363 average. The baseball world set him up to be the next Ted Williams, a Boston boy who could hit for average and slug homers, but Boggs only hit double digits one other time with 11 in 1994. His tendency to hit to the opposite field reduces his power.

Wade was traded to the Yankees in 1993, much to the dismay of the arch rival Red Sox. Even more frustrating for BoSox fans was that Boggs finally captured a World Series ring. His good fortune with the Yanks only adds to the mystique of "the Curse of the Bambino." At the end of 1997, at age 39, he was only 200 hits shy of the magic 3,000.

*B*oggs is one of the most superstitious men in baseball. He goes through the same pregame ritual every single day of the season. He eats chicken before every game. If he's in a slump, he has to eat fried chicken from a certain restaurant. He believes that if strawberries are put on his cheesecake, it's bad luck. It has to be plain. He draws the same pattern in the dirt with his toe before he steps into the batter's box, and he runs the exact same route out to third base every time he takes the field.

CAREER STATISTICS

Batting average	.331
At bats	8,453
Hits	2,800
Doubles	541
Triples	56
Home runs	109
Runs scored	1,422
Runs batted in	933
Walks	1,328

Barry Bonds

Barry Lamar Bonds is the San Francisco Giants left fielder. He's one of eight players in baseball history to win the MVP award three times, and he is the only one to do it in three out of four seasons, 1990, 1992, and 1993, respectively. In the fourth season (1991), he lost by only two votes. He and José Canseco are the only two players to have ever hit 40 home runs and stolen 40 bases in the same season.

Barry Bonds is the slugging, base-stealing superstar son of Bobby Bonds. While the apple doesn't fall far from the tree, the son now has the slight edge. He's had three seasons with 40 home runs or over, five batting over .300, and seven with over 100 RBIs, stats his father could only dream about.

Chip Off the Old Block

There are only four players in history who have hit 300 total home runs and stolen 300 total bases. The Bonds family takes up half of that list. Willie Mays is in first. Andre Dawson is in second. Bobby is in third, and Barry follows in fourth. But he's still playing, and he's playing well. By the end of his career, it's likely he will pass his father in both homers and stolen bases.

Barry plays for the San Francisco Giants, his hometown team. He signed with them as a free agent in 1992. He grew up about 20 miles from the park, a big fan of Willie Mays, who is his godfather. By the time he was four years old, he was a regular visitor at Candlestick Park. He would play catch with Mays and shag flies as the Giants took batting practice.

A Fan Undercover

When Barry was old enough, he starred on his little league team. Bobby wanted to watch his son play, but the attention he got in the stands was a distraction from the game. Instead, he used to pull his car up behind some trees and watch the game hidden from sight.

Barry also starred in football and basketball in high school, but baseball was his ticket to fame. He signed with Pittsburgh in 1985 after being chosen in the first round of the draft. He only spent one year in the minors before being brought up to the Pirates in 1986.

One of the ways Barry Bonds trains during the off-season is by using tennis balls. He puts numbers on the balls, and as the pitches fly at him from the machine, he tries to swing at only the odd-numbered ones.

Superstardom

His first real breakout year, however, was 1990. He hit .301, belted 33 home runs, knocked in 114 RBIs, and had 52 steals for his first 30-30 year (although it was more like a 30-50 year). He was voted the NL MVP, and it was the first year he was voted to the All-Star team.

In 1992 he had his second 30-30 year and second MVP award, hitting .311 with 34 home runs, 103 RBIs, and 39 stolen bases. He led the league in runs, walks, slugging average, and home run percentage as well.

It's hard to believe he could improve on that, but he did. When he joined the Giants in 1993, he got his third MVP award in four years. He led the league in homers, with 46 and RBIs with 123. His batting average of .336 was higher than any combination home run and RBI leader since 1937. Bonds joined the exclusive 40-40 club in 1996 and remains one of the biggest offensive threats in baseball. He smacked 40 more homers in 1997, leaving him 26 short of 400 for his career.

CAREER STATISTICS

Batting average	.288
At bats	6,069
Hits	1,750
Doubles	359
Triples	56
Home runs	374
Runs scored	1,244
Runs batted in	1,094
Walks	1,227

George Brett

George Howard Brett is eleventh on the all-time hit list. A member of the 3,000 hit club, he notched a total of 3,154 in his 21-year career. He's fifth on the all-time doubles list, with 665. He led the league in average three times, hits three times, triples three times, and doubles twice. He retired in 1993, with a lifetime average of .305.

A Loyal Royal

George Brett was Kansas City's franchise player. In an era where players jump from team to team to get the best salary or the most likely chance of winning, George Brett stayed put. He was the king of the Royals, the most popular player Kansas City ever had.

Although Brett was born in Glen Dale, West Virginia, he moved to Hermosa Beach, California, as a young child. He was the youngest of four boys in his family and, as far as baseball was concerned, thought to be the least-talented. The top player was George's brother Ken. Ken's high school pitching record was 33-3. Although he played in the majors for 12 years, he never became a superstar. George did.

He started his big league career slowly, getting a mere five hits in 40 at bats in 1973. But by the end of 1974, he'd secured his job as the Royals third baseman. Then he couldn't miss. In 1975 he led the league in hits, almost breaking the 200-mark with 195. He also led the league in triples that year. The next year he won his first batting crown with a .333 average and broke 200 with 215 hits, also tops in the league. Again, he led the league in triples, this time with 14.

The Magical .400 Mark

He had 212 hits in 1979 to lead the league, but his shining season came in 1980. In September of that year, he was batting .393. There was a chance that he could break the .400 mark, something that hadn't been done since Ted Williams hit .406 in 1941. But it was a long shot. Brett almost had to bat .500 for the last 11 games of the season. Unfortunately, he didn't make it. But he did end the season with a phenomenal .390 average.

George Brett is the only player in major league history to win a batting title in three different decades. Brett led the AL in 1976, 1980, and 1990.

Pitchers didn't know what to throw him. He could hit anything, high balls, low balls, inside strikes, outside strikes, fastballs, curve balls, and sliders. When asked what type of pitch he liked to look for, he answered, "I just look for the ball."

Brett averaged over .300, 11 of his 21 years. He also had 14 years of double-digit home runs, although he never thought of himself as a power-hitter. Twice he notched more than 200 hits in a season, and four times he brought in over 100 runs. Those cumulative stats would have been even higher if he hadn't been injured so much.

Down and Dirty

The Kansas City Royals play on Astroturf at home, which is hard on the body of a player like Brett who throws himself into every play. He had no regard for his body, and it showed. He went on the disabled list almost every year for a toe, a heel, ankles, knees, ribs, back, hands, wrists, or a shoulder. In his 21 seasons, there were only six where he played more than 150 games.

Brett ended up notching hit number 3,000 in October of 1993. He retired a year later, finishing with a total of 3,154.

CAREER STATISTICS	
Batting average	.305
At bats	10,349
Hits	3,154
Doubles	665
Triples	137
Home runs	317
Runs scored	1,583
Runs batted in	1,595
Walks	1,096

Lou Brock

Louis Clark Brock, once baseball's all-time leader in stolen bases, was also quite a hitter. He had four 200-hit seasons and retired as a member of the 3,000 hit club. His lifetime average was .293, and he was inducted into the Hall of Fame in 1985.

When the Chicago Cubs brought Lou Brock up to the majors, they weren't very impressed. He had two full seasons with them, both of which earned him averages in the mid .200s.

Wake-up Call

The St. Louis Cardinals picked him up relatively cheaply in a multiplayer trade. Brock exploded, hitting .348, helping St. Louis come from behind to win the pennant. They went on to win the World Series, where he batted .300 with nine hits and five RBIs.

Lou Brock then proceeded to have an amazing career. He had eight seasons over .300, scored over 90 runs ten times, and had four 200-hit seasons. He shined in World Series play. In 1967 Brock hit .414, and in the 1968 World Series he hit .464.

In 1978 it seemed as if his career might be over. He thought about retiring, but he didn't want to end on such a bad note. So at age 40, Brock returned to get his 3,000th hit and bat .304 on the season.

CAREER STATISTICS

Batting average	.293
At bats	10,332
Hits	3,023
Doubles	486
Triples	141
Home runs	149
Runs scored	1,610
Runs batted in	900
Walks	938

Roy Campanella

PLAYED 1948–1957

Roy "Campy" Campanella was the league's MVP three years during his ten-year career. He hit over 20 home runs in all but two years, hitting 41 of them in 1953. He was inducted into the Hall of Fame in 1969.

Roy Campanella was born on November 19, 1921, and grew up in Homestead, Pennsylvania. He delivered milk to help with the family income. But he stayed in school and starred in three sports, one of them being baseball.

The 27-Year-Old Rookie

When he was only 15, however, he joined the Baltimore Elites of the Negro Leagues. He played with them for the next nine years, but none of those stats count for his major league totals. Two years after Jackie Robinson broke in to the majors, the Brooklyn Dodgers signed Roy Campanella as their catcher.

Campanella didn't let the Dodgers down. He set records for catchers, won the MVP award three times, and helped them to five pennant wins. In 1953 he had his best season. He hit .312 with 41 home runs, led the league in RBIs with 142, and scored 103 runs.

After ten incredible years, tragedy struck. He was driving his car on an icy road when he lost control. He crashed and broke his neck. He was paralyzed and would never play ball again. He was inducted into the Hall of Fame in 1969.

CAREER STATISTICS

Batting average	.276
At bats	4,205
Hits	1,161
Doubles	178
Triples	18
Home runs	242
Runs scored	627
Runs batted in	856
Walks	533

José Canseco

*J*osé Canseco is the designated hitter for the Oakland Athletics. He has had five seasons with over 100 RBIs and 12 seasons with double-digit home runs. He became baseball's first ever 40-40 man with 42 home runs and 40 steals in a single season.

José Canseco and his twin brother, Ozzie, were born in Havana, Cuba, on July 2, 1964. His mother got sick with hepatitis from the birth, and she was sick with complications for the rest of her life. She died when José was nineteen.

A Late Bloomer

The Canseco's left Cuba a year after the twins were born and settled in Florida. José's parents were not sports people, so they didn't encourage their children to play. José didn't begin playing baseball until he was 13, and he didn't make the high school varsity team until he was a senior. He did well that year, though, playing third base and hitting .400.

Although nobody was much interested in this skinny Miami boy, a scout for the A's thought he might be worth taking a chance on. The A's drafted him in the 15th round of the 1982 draft. They got lucky.

In 1986, Canseco's first full season with the Athletics, he was voted Rookie of the Year. Although he set a new Oakland record for strikeouts, and his batting average was a dismal .240, he hit 33 home runs and had 117 RBIs.

Hit and Run

Two years later, Canseco had the year of his career. He hit over .300 and crushed 42 home runs. He knocked in over 100 RBIs for the third season in a row, and he stole 40 bases, becoming baseball's first ever 40-40 man. Barry Bonds has since joined him in that category. He was unanimously voted the MVP award, becoming only the seventh player, and the first since Reggie Jackson, to get all the votes.

Canseco played a major role in Oakland's success as the A's won three straight pennants from 1988 to 1990. Oakland advanced to the World Series each time, but won the world championship only once in 1989. Canseco and Mark McGwire were the major offensive weapons for the A's during their short dynasty.

José has always been a productive hitter, but his career has been hampered by injuries. In 1989 he hurt a bone in his hand. In 1990 he had a protruding disc in his lower back, forcing him to spend some time in traction. He was traded to Texas, and in 1993 while there he had surgery on his elbow. In 1995 he went to Boston, where he strained his groin muscle and hurt his ribs. And in 1996 he was out with hip problems and underwent back surgery after he ruptured a disc. He got married that year and had to take his vows from bed.

F rom 1987 to 1991 José Canseco and Mark McGwire were nicknamed "The Bash Brothers." They hit third and fourth in the Oakland lineup and were notorious for their monstrous tape-measure home runs. In 1987 Canseco and McGwire combined to hit 82 homers and launched 348 during their five-year span together in Oakland.

Still a Big Threat

The years he's been healthy, however, show that José still has what it takes to be a superstar. In 1991 he passed the 40 mark in homers again with 44, and in 1996 he again hit over .300, batting .307 with 24 home runs, and 84 RBIs.

Injuries have not been the only problems that José has had to deal with. He was accused of using steroids. He was arrested for having a gun hidden in his car (it's illegal in California). And he was stopped and given a huge fine for going 125 mph in his Jaguar. José seems to have gotten his life back together. His return to Oakland may be just what he needs to give his career a jump start.

CAREER STATISTICS

Batting average	.269
At bats	5,459
Hits	1,470
Doubles	270
Triples	13
Home runs	351
Runs scored	1,107
Runs batted in	920
Walks	674

Rod Carew

Rodney Cline Carew was one of the top average hitters in recent decades. He retired with a .328 average and 3,053 hits. He won seven batting titles and was inducted into the Hall of Fame in 1991.

Better than Average

Rod Carew was another hitter, like Ty Cobb, who felt that hitting for average was more important to the team than hitting for power. He made that his goal and had tremendous success. He had 15 seasons where his average was over .300 and six seasons where his strikeout numbers were in the single digits. During his impressive career, he captured the batting crown seven times, including six in seven years from 1972 to 1978.

Carew was born near the Panama Canal, but he moved to New York City when he was a teenager. After high school he was signed by the Twins, and shortly after that he won the Rookie of the Year award, batting .292. Then, for the next 15 seasons, he hit over .300, getting over 200 hits four times. In five of those seasons he hit over .350, once even reaching the lofty .388 mark. The baseball world thought of him as the best hope of a player ever breaking .400 again. But despite his consistency at the plate, it never happened.

A Wizard with the Wood

One of the reasons Rod Carew had such a high batting average was his amazing bunting ability. For him, the bunt was not a "sacrifice" hit. He had perfected it and often used it to get a base hit rather than hitting away. The big advantage to his bunting skill is that fielders never knew how to play him. If they came in close, he hit away. If they stayed back, he bunted. His control was so good that in practice he used to place handkerchiefs at various points on the foul lines, then drop bunts right on top of them!

Carew left Minnesota after the 1978 season to become a member of the California Angels. His presence had an immediate impact as the Angels won the AL Western Division title. They lost the league championship series to the Orioles in four games, despite Carew's lofty .412 batting average.

od Carew was so good at connecting with the ball that pitchers just couldn't get him out. Jim Palmer had a strategy, though. He would just throw the pitch and hope and pray that somebody fielded it.

Carew notched hit number 3,000 in 1985. It was an opposite field single, a fitting tribute to the type of hitter Carew was. He was inducted into the Hall of Fame in his first year of eligibility—only the 22nd player to ever achieve that.

Although his name is no longer found on major league lineup cards, Carew still makes life difficult for pitchers. He is currently the Anaheim Angels hitting instructor and helps young superstars like Tim Salmon and Jim Edmonds.

CAREER STATISTICS

Batting average	.328
At bats	9,315
Hits	3,053
Doubles	445
Triples	112
Home runs	92
Runs scored	1,424
Runs batted in	1,015
Walks	1,018

Joe Carter

*J*oseph Chris Carter is the Toronto Blue Jays left fielder and designated hitter. He has driven in over 100 runs ten times in his 13 full major league seasons. For the last 12 seasons, he's hit over 20 home runs, hitting at least 30 five times.*

The Mid-Western Kid

Joe Carter, all-around nice guy, was born on March 7, 1960, in Oklahoma City. He was one of ten children. He played four sports in high school, including baseball, basketball, football, and track, but baseball was clearly his best. He went to Wichita State for college and was drafted by the Chicago Cubs in 1981.

In 1983 Chicago brought him up for 23 games. His numbers were unimpressive and they promptly traded him to Cleveland. The Indians had gotten a sleeper. He hit 13 home runs for them in less than half a season. The next year he hit just 15, but he missed quite a few games due to injuries. By 1986 he belted out 29. That season was the first of many 100+ RBI seasons for Joe, and he led the league that year with 121.

On top of his slugging ability, Joe is fast. He became the Indians first ever 30-30 man, hitting over 32 home runs in the same season he stole 31 bases. He was also the third AL player in history to reach the 30-30 mark and also have 100 RBIs.

Canadian Champ

Despite his individual achievements, Joe never had the opportunity to play for a serious contender. Cleveland was still struggling as an organization and decided to unload him.

Joe was traded to the Padres in 1990, spending one career low year with them, and then he was traded to the Toronto Blue Jays. There, his luck finally changed as he led the Blue Jays to three division titles, two pennants, and two World Series titles.

Living a Fantasy

On October 23, 1993, in the sixth game of the World Series, Joe had the highlight of his career. The Blue Jays had won three games, the Philadelphia Phillies only two. In the ninth inning of game six, the Blue Jays were down 6-5 when Joe Carter came up to bat. There were two men on base and one out. Mitch Williams was on the mound. He threw the pitch, and Joe blasted it out of the park for a three-run homer that ended the game, giving the Blue Jays their second world championship. Carter jumped for joy as he circled the bases. His teammates greeted him at home plate in a wild celebration. He became only the second player in history to end the World Series with a homer. His bat went to the Hall of Fame. Joe kept the ball.

Although his offensive numbers have dipped the past few years, Carter is still a reliable RBI man. He drove in 102 runs in 1997 despite hitting just .234. If he performs well in 1998, he just may crack the 400th homer of his career.

Joe Carter has been involved in trades with both Alomar brothers. In 1989 he was traded to San Diego for Sandy Alomar, Chris James, and Carlos Baerga. In 1990 he was traded with Roberto Alomar to Toronto for Fred McGriff and Tony Fernandez.

CAREER STATISTICS

Batting average	.259
At bats	8,034
Hits	2,083
Doubles	410
Triples	52
Home runs	378
Runs scored	1,119
Runs batted in	1,382
Walks	503

Roberto Clemente

Roberto Walker Clemente is another member of the 3,000 hit club, with exactly 3,000. His lifetime batting average is .317. He took the batting title four times, and in 13 of his 18 seasons with Pittsburgh, he batted over .300. Roberto was inducted into the Hall of Fame in a special election in 1973.

Roberto Clemente was born in Puerto Rico. His father was the foreman at a sugar plantation, and the large family was fairly well-off. Roberto had a job unloading grocery trucks, which he claims helped build the muscles he needed for baseball. Even at that young age, it was clear that a career in baseball was in his future.

A Pirate at Heart

He signed on with a minor league team in Puerto Rico and did so well that he was snapped up by the Brooklyn Dodgers. A year later, Pittsburgh grabbed him in the draft. They never regretted it. Clemente played with the Pirates his entire career, hitting over .300 for 13 of his seasons, notching over 200 hits for four seasons, and winning the batting title four times. He led the Pirates to two spectacular seven-game World Series, one in 1960, the other in 1971. The Pirates won them both with Clemente hitting .310 and .414. In the 1971 series, he slugged two home runs and got a hit in every game.

He was a slashing line-drive hitter rather than a power hitter. The fences in Forbes Field, where the Pirates played, were deep. Clemente would have had to really work to become a home-run hitter. Most of his hits went to the opposite field. He stood far away from the plate so he could extend his arms on his swing. If the pitcher tried to throw the ball on the outside corner, Clemente would dive in and smash the ball to right-center field. But if he was pitched inside, he would just turn his hips and rip the ball to left field.

In the last game he would ever play, Clemente registered his 3,000th career hit. He also finished with 240 home runs. Who knows what his numbers would have been if not for chronic back problems and a career that was cut short by tragedy.

A Hall of Fame Citizen

Roberto Clemente was not only a great baseball player, he was also a truly great person. He was a role model for thousands of kids both on and off the field. When he died, he was building something he called "Sports City" in Puerto Rico. It was going to be a place where young kids could learn to play. He was also running Puerto Rico's efforts to help the Nicaraguans who had just been hit by a devastating earthquake.

Clemente also had tremendous fielding ability, with an incredibly powerful arm. He could throw from the right-field fence to the catcher on the fly. It was 460 feet away!

On December 31, 1972, he was taking emergency supplies to Nicaragua. Usually he didn't fly with the supplies, but this time he did because he thought that they were getting into the hands of the wrong people. It proved to be a fateful decision. The cargo plane he was riding in crashed into the ocean. There were no survivors. His three young sons lost their father, the world lost a great man, and baseball lost one of its top stars. But he had achieved one of his dreams. He once said, "I want to be remembered as a ballplayer who gave all he had to give."

An Express Enshrinement

Eleven weeks later, baseball decided to hold a special Hall of Fame election. Under normal circumstances, a player must be out of baseball for five years before he is eligible to be voted in. They didn't want to wait for Clemente. He was elected to the Hall of Fame with a whopping 93 percent of the vote.

CAREER STATISTICS	
Batting average	.317
At bats	9,454
Hits	3,000
Doubles	440
Triples	166
Home runs	240
Runs scored	1,416
Runs batted in	1,305
Walks	621

Ty Cobb

Many people will tell you that Tyrus Raymond Cobb was the greatest hitter to play the game. He holds the all-time record for batting average, with .367. He's also first in runs. He's second in hits and triples and fourth in doubles and RBIs. For all but one of the 13 years between 1907 and 1919, he captured the batting title. He was the top vote-getter on the first Hall of Fame ballot, beating out Babe Ruth and Honus Wagner.

Dead Ball Champ

Ty Cobb was the champion of the Dead Ball Era. In the early years of the 20th century, just as the AL was being formed, the baseballs that were used thudded off the bat. On top of that, pitchers were allowed to scuff, slice, and spit on the ball to make it tougher on the hitter. Home runs were scarce, so batters had to rely on careful hit placement, bunts, steals, and hit-and-run plays just to get around the bases. Ty Cobb was a master of all of these. Now, even with a ball that just jumps off the bat, nobody can come close to Cobb's numbers. Players rarely average in a season what he averaged in a lifetime. His .367 career batting average is likely to stand forever.

And that's just the beginning. Cobb notched nine 200-hit seasons. Three years he batted over .400. Starting in his second year, and for 22 years after that, Cobb batted over .300. He even managed to take the triple crown in 1909, with a .377 average, nine home runs, and 107 RBIs, and he never even wanted to be thought of as a power hitter.

Chief Thief

On top of that he was an extraordinary base-stealer, retiring at number one in that category in both season and career totals. But he was also caught stealing a huge number of times. Cobb claimed that he often stole when he knew he'd be caught, just to get a reputation for running at any crazy time. This rattled pitchers and fielders alike whenever Cobb got on base, and often they were paying more attention to him than the batter. But despite this outlandish philosophy, he really could run. More than once he got on first and then stole second, third, and home. When asked what he did when he saw Cobb stealing second, one catcher replied, "I throw to third."

Cobb spent the first 22 years of his incredible career as a Detroit Tiger. The players who took the field with him described him as possessed, obsessed, mean, and fiery. He was a Southerner to the core, and playing in the North-dominated major leagues, he seemed to embody the South's rebel reputation. He took It personally when his teammates teased him as a rookie, and he never got over it.

Ty Cobb hated Babe Ruth and the way his slugging changed the game of baseball. Cobb thought it took a lot more skill and was a lot more interesting to hit the ball in the gaps. In 1925 Cobb announced he would be a power hitter for two games to prove how easy it was to hit home runs. In the first game, he hit three home runs. In the second game he hit two. Satisfied that he had proved his point, he went back to slapping singles.

Controlling His Destiny

Even though he might shoot off at the mouth when he was off the field, at the plate he had great control. He was thinking at every at bat. He would bunt if the infield was deep, slap it over their heads if they came in. Walter Johnson, one of the all-time greatest pitchers couldn't get Cobb out because he crowded the plate on him. Cobb knew that Johnson was a nice guy and wouldn't want to hit anybody, so he made Johnson pitch wide. Johnson either ended up walking Cobb or he eased up on his fastball to make sure he got it over the plate, and then Cobb drove that easier pitch into the field for a single. Charles Comiskey, the legendary owner of the White Sox, once said of him, "[He] is able to respond better than any other player to any demand made upon him."

You'd think with his record Ty Cobb would be held up as an example of great hitting by coaches everywhere. Not even close. Cobb had a very strange grip. He split his hands, so at times there were as many

as four inches between the top and the bottom. His swing was restricted, but it did give him that incredible control to bunt, punch, or slap the ball, a style that served him well in the Dead Ball Era. And it would be unfair to say that his remarkable skill just came to him naturally. Cobb worked harder than anyone to perfect his game. If a pitch had bothered him in the previous day's game, he would be out working on it the next day. He never let up.

Nasty Character

Off the field, however, he seemed to have no control. Virtually no one liked him. He humiliated people, insulted them, and generally alienated everyone around him. Some people attributed this to his obsessive need to be the best at everything.

One of the few times Cobb seemed to take the high road was when the 1910 batting title was in dispute. Ironically, it was the one year the Chalmers Automobile Company was offering a free car to the winner. The country was desperate for the "nice guy" Napoleon Lajoie to win. The St. Louis Browns, who also wanted Lajoie to win, gave away eight easy hits to Lajoie, which put him at the top. Cobb's only comment was that he was sorry the title couldn't have been won by either one of them without an incident to mar the moment. Lajoie's "gift hits" were taken away, Cobb was reinstated as the leader, and Chalmers ended up taking the high road, too. Both men got a car.

A Short Fuse

But Cobb's temper could not be suppressed for long. In 1912 he leapt into the stands to beat up a disabled man who was taunting him. Cobb kept kicking him with his spikes until he was pulled off the man. This time, he was suspended from the game by Ban Johnson, the president of the AL. Cobb's teammates felt that his suspension was unreasonably harsh and refused to play. Cobb was reinstated, but he and his teammates had to pay a fine.

Finally, in 1926, he was suspended again. This time he was accused of fixing a game with Tris Speaker. Cobb fought the charge. Some say that the pitcher who made the accusation was scared of Cobb and backed off. Other people, including Cobb and Speaker, claim the man was just out to get them and had no evidence. Whatever the reason, the charges were dropped and Cobb returned to baseball. He came back this time as a member of the Philadelphia Athletics and put up his typical great numbers for two more seasons.

When Cobb was 18, three weeks before his big league career took off, a tragedy occurred. Cobb's mother was alone in the house. Cobb's father had said he wouldn't be back until very late that night, possibly even the next day, so when Mrs. Cobb saw a man trying to get into her house, she assumed it was an intruder and shot him. In fact, it was Cobb's father, and he died immediately.

Big Regret

But his legs were shot, and it was time to retire. He retired with a reputation for being the game's best hitter, and he retired a rich man. He had been paid well, and he'd invested quite a bit in a small soft drink company in Georgia that was to become even more famous than Cobb: Coca-Cola. But despite all his achievements, Cobb and the Detroit Tigers only went to the World Series once, in 1909. And they lost. It's Cobb's biggest regret that he wasn't on a World Champion team.

CAREER STATISTICS	
Batting average	.367
At bats	11,429
Hits	4,191
Doubles	724
Triples	297
Home runs	118
Runs scored	2,245
Runs batted in	1,961
Walks	1,249

Mickey Cochrane

Gordon Stanley "Mickey" Cochrane was a Hall of Fame catcher for the Philadelphia Athletics and later the Detroit Tigers. His lifetime hitting average of .320 still holds the record for catchers. Although he only played for 12 years, he went to the World Series five times.

Fire in the Dugout

Mickey Cochrane's hothead personality further extended his fame. He took every loss personally and was often called "Black Mike" because of the foul moods that an error, a strikeout, or a loss might put him into. But if he demanded perfection from himself and others, it seemed to work. Not only was he the top catcher in the game, but his team ran away with the 1929 World Series. Cochrane batted .400 in the World Series, and the team set a record by scoring ten runs in one inning.

His career might have gone on longer, but in May of 1937 he was hit in the head by Yankee pitcher Bump Hadley. The beaning knocked him out, put him in the hospital, and was nearly the end of him. When he finally did recover, he was eager to get back into baseball, but the owner of the Tigers wouldn't allow it. The doctors warned that another blow to the head would end his life. So Cochrane ended his playing career and managed the team for a year and a half.

CAREER STATISTICS	
Batting average	.320
At bats	5,169
Hits	1,652
Doubles	333
Triples	64
Home runs	118
Runs scored	1,041
Runs batted in	832
Walks	857

Eddie Collins

Eighth on the all-time hit list with 3,313 hits, Eddie "Cocky" Collins dominated the game of baseball through the first quarter of the 20th century. In 18 of his 25 seasons, he batted over .300 and retired with a .333 average. He was inducted into the Hall of Fame in 1939.

Even though Eddie Collins was too young to play in the first six years of the 20th century, at 19 he couldn't wait anymore. He entered the game while still in college in 1906 and didn't stop for 25 years, when he retired at age 43. He began and ended his career with the Philadelphia Athletics, with a 12-year stint on the Chicago White Sox sandwiched in the middle.

In his 25 years as a ballplayer, Collins never won a batting title, but he hit over .300 in 18 of the seasons, over .340 in ten. And hitting wasn't the only thing he could do. According to some, he was the best second baseman the game had ever seen, and that, combined with his hitting and base stealing (fourth on the all-time list), allowed him to lead six of his teams to the World Series. He batted over .400 in three of those series.

One of those teams was the 1919 Chicago White Sox team that lost the World Series on purpose. Eddie was the unofficial leader of the "innocent" ballplayers, those who were unaware of the scam. His reputation never suffered from the scandal, but he never forgave the players who were involved.

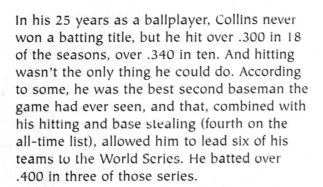

CAREER STATISTICS

Batting average	.333
At bats	9,951
Hits	3,313
Doubles	438
Triples	187
Home runs	47
Runs scored	1,820
Runs batted in	1,300
Walks	1,503

Earle Combs

*E*arle Combs was the Yankee center fielder from 1924 to 1935, leadoff hitter of the famous "Murderer's Row." He retired with a lifetime batting average of .325. In three seasons he amassed over 200 hits, leading the league once. And he topped the charts in triples three times.

Setting the Table

It's often said that Babe Ruth's performances often left Lou Gehrig in the shadows, so you can imagine how Earle Combs must have felt playing with both of them. He was the leadoff hitter for the Yankees' incredible hitting squad, known to many fans as "Murderer's Row." Even though his accomplishments are sometimes overlooked, he was often the one leading the team in hits. In 1927 he led the entire league with 231 of them.

In his rookie season Combs was batting .400 when he broke his ankle. He was out for the rest of the year, but he picked up where he left off. Combs finished 1925 with a .342 average. He had 203 hits, including 13 triples. Those triples eventually became his hallmark. He didn't have the power to hit home runs (the Yankees had their fair share, anyway), but he did have the speed to pace the league in triples in 1927, 1928, and 1930.

CAREER STATISTICS

Batting average	.325
At bats	5,748
Hits	1,866
Doubles	309
Triples	154
Home runs	58
Runs scored	1,186
Runs batted in	629
Walks	670

Andre Dawson

*A*ndre *"the Hawk" Dawson hit double-digit home runs for 18 straight seasons and smacked over 20 homers in 13 of them. He won the NL MVP award in 1987 and retired with 438 lifetime homers.*

Andre Nolan Dawson was born on July 10, 1954, in Miami, Florida. His nickname was "the Hawk" because of his predatory glare out toward the pitcher's mound. Dawson was a well-rounded player, hitting for power, stealing bases, and winning eight gold glove awards.

Dawson got his first taste of the major leagues with the Montreal Expos. He played in just 24 games in 1976 but earned a starting spot the following season, hitting .282 with 19 homers. Dawson became a dominant force in the Expos lineup during the 1970s and teamed with Gary Carter to lead Montreal to their first postseason appearance in 1981. He hit .301 and swiped 39 bases in 1982, and smacked 32 home runs while leading the league in hits with 189 the following season.

In 1987 Dawson signed with the Chicago Cubs as a free agent and had a career-best season. He led the league in homers (49) and RBIs (137) and won the NL MVP award. In 1990 he joined Willie Mays and Bobby Bonds as one of only three players to hit 300 home runs and steal 300 bases in a career. Barry Bonds has since joined that elite club. Dawson signed with the Boston Red Sox in 1993 and retired with the Florida Marlins following the 1996 season.

CAREER STATISTICS

Batting average	.279
At bats	9,927
Hits	2,774
Doubles	503
Triples	98
Home runs	438
Runs scored	1,373
Runs batted in	1,591
Walks	587

Bill Dickey

William Malcolm Dickey was an all-around top hitter. He consistently hit over .300, while also smacking over 20 home runs and driving in over 100 RBIs during his peak years. He set an all-time record for a catcher, batting .362 in 1936, and he retired with a .313 overall average.

Bill Dickey has always been considered one of the best catchers baseball has ever seen. His defensive skill behind the plate and his consistent excellence when he stepped up to it combined to make him one of the game's top players. He was also Lou Gehrig's closest friend and roommate.

A Streak of His Own

Bill Dickey played all 17 years of his career with the New York Yankees. And these were the Yankees in their prime. Dickey competed in eight World Series, and he and the Yankees won seven of them! In those eight series, Dickey caught every inning of every game. It was his home run in the final game of the 1943 World Series that gave the Yankees the championship.

Right after that season Dickey enlisted in the Navy, doing his part in World War II. He came back to baseball in 1946, but his career was essentially over. He was voted into the Hall of Fame in 1984.

CAREER STATISTICS

Batting average	.313
At bats	6,300
Hits	1,969
Doubles	343
Triples	72
Home runs	202
Runs scored	930
Runs batted in	1,209
Walks	678

Joe DiMaggio

PLAYED 1936–1951

Joseph Paul "Joltin' Joe" DiMaggio still holds the record for hitting safely in 56 consecutive games. In all but two seasons, he batted over .300 and retired with a lifetime average of .325. He had double-digit home run totals every year of his career, and he led the league twice each in average, home runs, and RBIs.

Joltin' Joe DiMaggio, also called the Yankee Clipper, played center field for the Yankees for 13 years. In ten of those years he brought the Bronx Bombers to the World Series. He's fourth on the list for total World Series hits, and seventh for home runs.

Poetry in Motion

Although the war ensured that his stats would never be at the top, many consider him the greatest all-around baseball player. There was nothing he couldn't do. His manager, Joe McCarthy, was once asked if DiMaggio could bunt. McCarthy replied, "I don't know, nor do I have any intention of finding out."

Joseph Paul DiMaggio was born in California on November 25, 1914, the middle of three baseball playing brothers and the eighth of nine children. Their parents, Italian immigrants, weren't too enthusiastic about their obsession with baseball. It was especially painful when Joe dropped out of high school to play baseball. For a while he worked with his father on the docks at Fisherman's Wharf in San Francisco, but the call of the diamond was too much. His persistence paid off.

Seal of Approval

He began his professional career with the San Francisco Seals at 17. He turned in a tremendous performance in his second year, hitting .340, with 28 home runs and 169 RBIs. There was little doubt where he was headed. The next year, however, he hurt his knee.

When Joe started in the minors, he played shortstop, but after eleven wild throws in one game they moved him to center field.

Not as many teams were pursuing him as he'd hoped. But the Yankees were willing to give him a chance. They left him in San Francisco one more year, and after he hit .398 with 34 home runs and 154 RBIs, he'd earned himself a starting position in New York.

He didn't disappoint the Yankee fans. His first year in the Bronx, he hit .323, with 29 homers and 125 RBIs, and he led the league in triples. DiMaggio was one of the big reasons the Yankees became World Champions that year. The next year he led the league in home runs with 46, and again the Yankees won the World Series. In 1939, 1940, and 1941 he hit .381, .352, and .357, respectively, earning two batting crowns, two MVP awards, and two more World Series rings in the three years.

DiMaggio was a very private person off the field and didn't always enjoy being in the spotlight. He rarely was seen out in the public like Babe Ruth, and he didn't enjoy the extra media attention like Reggie Jackson. When DiMaggio married movie star Marilyn Monroe, however, his privacy all but disappeared. Luckily for the Yanks, any distractions in his personal life never affected his playing the game.

Not Your Average Joe

In 1941 Joe DiMaggio achieved his greatest accomplishment. On May 15 he went 1-for-4 against the Chicago White Sox. It was the beginning of a hitting streak that would last for 56 games. He first broke the Yankee consecutive game record of 29 that was set by Roger Peckinpaugh. Ironically, the day he tied it, he was playing against the Indians who Peckinpaugh managed. Then, on June 29 he first tied, then broke, George Sisler's AL record of 41 during a double header. In between the two games, a souvenir-seeking fan stole his bat. DiMaggio was worried, but it didn't matter. After four more games, he topped Wee Willie Keeler for the all-time record. Then it was just a matter of how long Joe could keep going.

Finally, the streak ended on July 17 in a game against the Cleveland Indians. Twice in that game he connected with pitches that could easily have gotten him a hit elsewhere, but the incredible fielding by Cleveland third baseman Ken Keltner put a stop to the streak. Amazingly enough, the very next day DiMaggio began another streak for 17 games.

A Tough One to Whiff

DiMaggio's feats are almost too numerous to mention. He almost never struck out. His highest strikeout total was in his first year, and even then it was only 39 times. He also managed to hit three homers in a game three times. And once he hit two home runs in the same inning of a game.

Unfortunately, as it did with other great players, World War II stepped in and stole three years from DiMaggio's career. His lifetime home-run tally is 361. Who knows what it might have been if he had been able to play those three more years in the prime of his career.

In 1947 DiMaggio won his third MVP award by one vote over Ted Williams. His numbers, while impressive, were not quite at the MVP level in the minds of many. He'd hit .315, knocked in 97 RBIs, and slugged 20 homers. That same year Ted Williams won the Triple Crown, hitting .343, with 114 RBIs and 32 home runs. But the Yankees went to the World Series, and the Red Sox stayed at Fenway.

Joe DiMaggio was a shy, quiet person. After games he would sit forever in the clubhouse to avoid fans. He would order room service instead of going out with teammates. According to Hank Greenberg, "If he said hello to you, that was a long conversation."

Back with a Bang

A heel injury and pneumonia cut down on DiMaggio's playing time in 1949. He didn't enter the lineup until a June doubleheader. The fans welcomed him back, and Joltin' Joe gave them a show. He went 5-for-11 in the two games and hit four home runs. Not surprisingly, the Yankees were off to another World Championship.

Joe DiMaggio always gave his best, even when he was in tremendous pain. And if the pain was too great, he took himself out of the lineup. He was not going to go out on the field and turn in half a performance. He was proud of his ability and didn't want his reputation hurt. "There's always some kid who may be seeing me for the first or last time. I owe him my best."

Joe had two more seasons—and two more World Series—with the Yankees, but then his injuries became too much. In 1951 he called it quits. He was inducted into the Hall of Fame in 1955.

CAREER STATISTICS

Batting average	**.325**
At bats	**6,821**
Hits	**2,214**
Doubles	**389**
Triples	**131**
Home runs	**361**
Runs scored	**1,390**
Runs batted in	**1,537**
Walks	**790**

Cecil Fielder

Cecil Grant "Big Daddy" *Fielder is the Yankee first baseman and designated hitter. He swings for the fences and has had tremendous success in the home run and RBI categories. In the seven years that he's had a full-time job in the majors, he's had six seasons with over 30 home runs and five seasons with over 100 RBIs.*

There are a lot of hitters in the game today who can do a lot of things for your team. Tony Gwynn can hit for high average, Kenny Lofton can hit for average and steal bases, and Barry Bonds can do it all. But if you want someone in your lineup whose job is to strictly hit the long ball, you want Big Daddy.

In the first three years of the decade, Fielder led the league twice in home runs, with 51 in 1990 and 44 in 1991, and three times in RBIs. Each season he had at least 120 RBIs.

Cecil was not an instant hit in the major leagues. He came up with the Toronto Blue Jays in 1985. He played part-time through 1988, never hitting more than 14 home runs in a season. In 1989 Fielder went to play in Japan to sharpen his skills. His specific goal was to learn how to hit curve balls.

The trip overseas seemed to pay off, as Fielder returned to play with the Detroit Tigers and hit 51 homers in 1990. Going into the final game of the season Fielder had 49 home runs and needed just one more to reach the 50 dinger plateau. He left his mark on history by hitting not one, but two out of the ball park. That's doing it in style.

Although Cecil's numbers dropped a little as the decade reached the halfway point, he stayed in the race. The strike-shortened year was the only year he didn't reach the 30-mark in home runs. And in 1996 he had another great year as he left Detroit to join the Yankees, banging out 39 homers and driving in 117 RBIs for the eventual world champions.

Heavy Hitter

Cecil Fielder's chop swing looks like Babe Ruth's, and so does his body. He weighs around 250 pounds, and he uses his size well, putting all his weight behind every swing. As most great hitters know, however, his real power comes from the speed he gets as he whips the bat across the plate.

Cecil Fielder first started playing baseball when he was seven. He tried it for one season and thought it was boring, so he stopped. He didn't pick it up again until his junior year in high school.

But speed in general is rare for Cecil. He's not a speedster on the bases or on first base. Nonetheless, he took his name off the record books for most games played without a stolen base by swiping his first one on April 2, 1996. He made it to second safely, most likely because everyone was too dumbfounded to make the play. But with his power, speed isn't really an issue. Cecil knocks the ball over the wall so many times, he just needs to learn to trot around the bases.

Fielder broke a bone in his hand at the beginning of the 1997 season, so his playing time was limited. But while he was on the disabled list, he lost 25 pounds and now looks as dangerous as ever. Despite his short season, Fielder managed to crack his 300th career homer.

CAREER STATISTICS

Batting average	.257
At bats	4,741
Hits	1,216
Doubles	183
Triples	6
Home runs	302
Runs scored	695
Runs batted in	940
Walks	640

Jimmie Foxx

James Emory Foxx was known for his slugging, but he still hit over .300 for nearly every year of his career, capturing the batting title twice. He had 12 consecutive years where he hit over 30 round-trippers. He's fourth on the all-time list for slugging percentage, sixth for RBIs, and ninth for home runs. When he retired, he was second in home runs, with 534, behind only Babe Ruth. Foxx was inducted into the Hall of Fame in 1951.

Jimmie Foxx, a Maryland farm boy, was discovered by Home Run Baker, the former Philadelphia A's third baseman. Even though the Yankees were interested in Foxx, Baker sent him along to Connie Mack out of loyalty to his old team. Many people wonder what the Yankees would have been like with Ruth, Gehrig, and Foxx. The A's, however, had their own impressive lineup with Mickey Cochrane, Al Simmons, and Foxx.

Showing His Guns

Foxx was one of the strongest sluggers to play the game, and it showed in his bulging arm muscles. He cut off his sleeves to display them. One player described them as looking like they'd been blown up with air. Another said "even his hair has muscles." Foxx's strength was legendary. He once hit a ball into the second to last row of Yankee stadium and broke a seat! He also hit one over the roof in Comiskey Park into a playground across the street.

He never broke any of Babe Ruth's records, always coming in second, but he still managed to lead the league in home runs four times in his career. This was not easy because he was playing at the same time and in the same league as Ruth. In 1932 he came the closest to Ruth's single-season record, smashing 58 homers over the fence. But he didn't seem to care. That was also the year he made a conscious effort to draw more walks (116). Late in the season during the month of August he hurt his wrist, which means that he would have had a very good chance at breaking Ruth's record.

A New Monster at Fenway

Because he was right-handed, he didn't have the advantage of the short right-field fences that most left-handed sluggers had. When he was traded to Boston in 1936, however, he got his turn with the Green Monster in Fenway Park. In six of his seven years with Boston, he hit over 30 home runs, leading the league twice. In 1938 he hit 50 home runs, but was second to Hank Greenberg, who hit 58.

He won the triple crown in 1933, batting .356, with 48 homers and 163 RBIS. He would have won it the year before, too, if the modern triple crown rules were in effect, but he came in second in the batting average to Dale Alexander, who only had 392 at bats. Foxx retired in 1945 and was inducted into the Hall of Fame in 1951.

From 1928 to 1930, Foxx and the A's replaced the Yanks as the best team in the AL. They went to the World Series three straight years, and won it all in 1928 and 1929. Foxx never hit lower than .333 in World Series play and had a career postseason slugging percentage of .609.

When his career as a player ended in 1945, largely because of his drinking and failing eyesight, Jimmie Foxx moved into coaching. But it wasn't a big league team he coached. He headed up Fort Wayne Daisies, one of the new All-American Girls Professional Baseball League teams that was formed when most of the country's young men were off fighting World War II.

CAREER STATISTICS

Batting average	.325
At bats	8,134
Hits	2,646
Doubles	458
Triples	125
Home runs	534
Runs scored	1,751
Runs batted in	1,921
Walks	1,452

Lou Gehrig

Henry Louis "the Iron Horse" Gehrig was part of the Ruth-Gehrig one-two punch of Murderer's Row. In his 17-year career, he hit over .300 14 times and launched more than 20 home runs 13 times. He led the league in every hitting category at least once and set a record for consecutive games played that lasted until 1995. He also set the record for career grand slams with 23. He was inducted into the Hall of Fame in 1939.

Lou Gehrig was born Ludwig Heinrich Gehrig in 1903 in New York City. He was the only one of his parents' children to survive childhood. His parents had big dreams for their only boy. Since Lou's father was a fraternity caretaker at Columbia University, they hoped that one day their son would get his education from the Ivy League school. Initially, it looked as if that was going to happen. Lou enrolled in Columbia as a freshman, playing baseball and football. There was one problem, however. He tried to play professionally at the same time, using Lewis as his fake name. He might have gotten away with it, but his skills were so obvious that he was soon noticed. Fortunately, he was noticed by the Yankees, who gave him so much money that he quit college and went to play with New York full-time.

A Sure Thing

The Yankees, however, didn't think he was quite ready for the bigs yet. They sent him to the minors until 1925. That's when "The Streak" started. On June 1 of that year, Gehrig was brought in to pinch hit for the second string first baseman. On June 2 the starting first baseman was beaned in the head by a pitch. Gehrig took over. On June 3 Gehrig made the position his own. For the next 2,127 games the Yankee lineup card always had Lou Gehrig's name penciled in. Gehrig had begun his 2,130 consecutive game streak.

Never Say Never

The streak was one that no one ever thought would be broken (it was, by Cal Ripken in 1995), and it was a record that fit Lou Gehrig perfectly. He was quiet and consistent. He never sought the limelight, which was a convenient trait for a hitter playing first behind Ruth and later behind DiMaggio.

But Gehrig's accomplishments weren't limited to his durability. Almost every year of his career he hit over 20 home runs and finished with an average over .300. But what is really remarkable is that he hit *over 40* home runs five times in his career and batted *over .350* six times. He won the Triple Crown in 1934, batting .363, hitting 49 homers, and driving in 165 RBIs. Except for his first year, he never had less than 100 runs or RBIs. He led in RBIs five times, runs four times, walks three times, homers three times, doubles twice, slugging average twice, hits once, and batting average once. The only hitting category he never topped was strikeouts. It doesn't get much better than that.

Even without Ruth to steal the spotlight, Gehrig's accomplishments were still overshadowed. Once he hit an incredible three triples in his first three at bats. The game was rained out. On the day that he became the first player ever to hit four home runs in a game, the legendary Giants owner John McGraw announced his retirement. McGraw got the baseball headlines on the front page. Gehrig's achievement was buried deep in the paper.

One feature that made Gehrig such a great hitter was that he was able to hit to all fields. Power hitters are notorious for pulling pitches with regularity, but Gehrig was anything but ordinary. This helped him in two different ways. First, there was no way to pitch him. Inside or outside, high or low, Gehrig made solid contact wherever the ball was thrown. In addition, defenses didn't know where to play him. If they moved over toward right field, he might hit it to left and vice versa. This ability allowed Gehrig to hit his home runs, but also hit for high average as well.

The Man Behind Ruth

Despite all his accomplishments, he was often overlooked in favor of Ruth. Gehrig hit 47 home runs in 1927 and beat Babe Ruth in both batting average and RBIs. But Ruth hit 60 homers, so he got the spotlight. In 1931 Gehrig tied Ruth for the home run title with 46. But he'd actually had 47 that year. One didn't count. He was tagged out for passing the base runner in front of him, who made the mistake of running off the field rather than crossing the plate. And guess who hit *three* homers in the 1932 World Series, including one immediately after Ruth's called shot. You guessed it. Gehrig.

A Born Winner

But Gehrig still had his share of fame. He and the Yankees went to seven World Series, winning six of them. There's an ongoing argument over which Yankee dynasty was more potent, the 1926–1928 crew, or the one a decade later. Gehrig was the only link between the two. He had a series average of .361, and in the 1928 and 1932 contests, he hit over .500! He also managed to slug ten homers and bring in 35 RBIs.

In 1938 Gehrig seemed to be having an off year. His numbers dipped, but they weren't far enough off for anyone to be concerned. In fact, for most hitters an average of .295, with 29 home runs would be considered a great year. But for Gehrig, it was the first time he was below .300 since his first year and the first time in ten years that his home run total was under 30.

An Unlucky Break

The next year, 1939, it was even worse. He just couldn't seem to get it together. His hitting and fielding were off. On May 2 he took himself out of the lineup for the first time in 14 years. A few weeks later, after trying to play in an exhibition game, he took off for the Mayo Clinic to find out what was wrong. They came back with a devastating diagnosis: Gehrig had amyotrophic lateral sclerosis. It meant that his spinal cord was hardening. It was a

Gehrig's manager, Joe McCarthy, would not break his string of consecutive games even when Gehrig was not performing as well as he should have been. He said the Gehrig would know when to call it quits. He wouldn't want to let the team down. That is exactly what happened. As Gehrig said, "McCarthy has been swell about it all the time. He'd let me go until the cows came home . . . but I knew in Sunday's game that I should get out of there."

rare disease, and there was no cure. Lou Gehrig did not have long to live, let alone play baseball.

He retired from baseball officially on July 4, 1939. The stadium was packed. Hoards of older Yankees that Gehrig had played with returned for the ceremony. As he watched them take the field in front of him he was choked up with emotion. In true Lou Gehrig form, his words showed his appreciation—of his friends, his fans, and his opportunity to play baseball. The speech will be remembered forever. "For the past two weeks, you've been reading about a bad break I got. Yet today I consider myself the luckiest man on the face of the earth."

They inducted Lou Gehrig into the Hall of Fame that year, instead of waiting for the traditional five years. He died two years later on June 2, 1941.

CAREER STATISTICS

Batting average	.340
At bats	8,001
Hits	2,721
Doubles	535
Triples	162
Home runs	493
Runs scored	1,888
Runs batted in	1,990
Walks	1,508

Charlie Gehringer

PLAYED 1924-1942

Charles Leonard "the Mechanical Man" Gehringer was a second baseman for the Detroit Tigers for 19 years. He has a lifetime batting average of .320. His 60 doubles in 1936 is still the record for the most doubles in a season by a second baseman.

A Tiger's Daily Duties

Charlie Gehringer was called "The Mechanical Man" for good reason. Every day he came to the ballpark and turned out a great performance, both as a nearly flawless second baseman and as a hitter. Until the final two years before he retired, he hit over .300 every year but one. That year, 1932, he hit .298. He also had seven seasons where he totalled 200 or more hits. Gehringer was a pure hitter.

Gehringer had three outstanding seasons that really turned him into a superstar. In 1929 he led the league in hits, double, triples, runs, and stolen bases. In 1936 he set his still-standing second baseman's record of 60 doubles. And in 1937 he hit .371, winning the AL batting title.

Though it may sound strange, Gehringer had an approach to hitting that helped him focus. He tried not to swing until he had two strikes. This way, he always made the pitcher work and got a good look at his pitches.

CAREER STATISTICS

Batting average	.320
At bats	8,860
Hits	2,839
Doubles	574
Triples	146
Home runs	184
Runs scored	1,774
Runs batted in	1,427
Walks	1,185

Josh Gibson

Josh Gibson was one of the most famous players of the Negro Leagues, right up there with pitcher Satchel Paige. He was considered the home run king of the league, and he had a lifetime batting average over .350. He was inducted into the Hall of Fame in 1972.

Josh Gibson was the biggest hitter to come out of the Negro Leagues. It's hard to say exactly what his numbers were because not all the records were kept.

Baseball's Record King?

Some "best guesses" have Josh Gibson breaking nearly every record in the major leagues. Some say his lifetime average was .390, breaking Ty Cobb's. Others say it was a mere .362. Some say Josh Gibson hit 84 homers in one season, beating out Roger Maris's 61. But is that with the exhibition games? And some say he hit a total of 962 home runs in his career, which would absolutely crush Hank Aaron's record of 755.

Nonetheless, Josh Gibson compiled a .412 batting average when he played against the major league players in exhibition games. In one game, he hit a grand slam off of Dizzy Dean. As much as he proved himself, however, he was never allowed to play in the major leagues.

CAREER STATISTICS	
Batting average	.362
At bats	1,679
Hits	607
Doubles	89
Triples	35
Home runs	146
Runs scored	N/A
Runs batted in	N/A
Walks	N/A

N/A = Complete statistics are not available

Juan Gonzalez

Juan Alberto "Igor" Gonzalez is the right fielder for the Texas Rangers. He's had double-digit home runs for every full year he's played, all but one year over 20. He's hit over 100 RBIs in every year but two. He has been the league's season home run leader three times.

Cream of the Crop

Juan Gonzalez won the AL MVP award in 1996. His batting average was .314, a career high for him. He slugged 47 home runs and drove in 144 RBIs. He did all this and missed almost a month while he was on the disabled list when he tore a quad muscle. He was the winner, but the race was so tight he could have used the extra month to beef up his stats even more. He barely beat out Alex Rodriguez, Albert Belle, Ken Griffey Jr., and Mo Vaughn for the title. It was the second tightest MVP voting in history, with the famous one-point Ted Williams/Joe DiMaggio battle in 1947.

Gonzalez was signed in by the Texas Rangers in 1986. He was a 17-year-old outfielder from Puerto Rico and weighed only 175 pounds. He started off slowly in the minors, but in 1989 his career started taking off. He began to add muscle to his frame through weight training and was called up to the big leagues at the end of the season. He had a brief stint with the Rangers again in 1990, and in 1991 he was in the major leagues to stay.

Man-made Power Hitter

His career has been littered with home run accomplishments. In 1992 and 1993 he led the AL in that category with 43 and 46. He was the first AL player since Jim Rice to lead the league in homers in back-to-back years.

Gonzalez is one of three active players (the other two are Frank Thomas and Ken Griffey Jr.) to have three 40 + homer seasons in the past five years. He and Griffey have now done it four times in the past six years. He is the only Ranger ever to reach that mark and is the only Ranger ever to have even one 40 homer season.

In 1995 he hit 27 homers, which doesn't sound remarkable until it's combined with his stat of 90 games played. To hit 27 home runs in a little over half a season is remarkable. At that pace he might have broken the 50-mark. The 47 he hit the next year certainly don't deny the possibility.

*D**uring his first year of minor league baseball, Juan Gonzalez hit no home runs. The next season he hit only eight homers in the Florida State League. Gonzalez worked hard in the weight room to become the masher he is today.*

In his only postseason appearance in 1996, Gonzalez put on an incredible performance. Although the Rangers lost to the New York Yankees in four games, Gonzalez hit five homers. He batted .438 and tied the major league record for home runs in a division series.

Once again in 1997 an injury stopped him from having a full season. A thumb injury in spring training kept him out of the lineup for the first month of 1997. He again put up extraordinary numbers for the amount of time he played. He smashed 42 homers in 533 at bats. He hit .296 and drove in 131 runs. The baseball world is still waiting to see what Gonzalez will do with 162 games.

CAREER STATISTICS

Batting average	.285
At bats	3,663
Hits	1,045
Doubles	196
Triples	16
Home runs	256
Runs scored	567
Runs batted in	790
Walks	247

Hank Greenberg

Henry Benjamin "Hammerin' Hank" Greenberg had eight seasons where he hit over .300. He led the league in home runs four times (tied a fifth), RBIs four times, and doubles twice. He is fifth on the all-time list for slugging percentage, with .605. He was inducted into the Hall of Fame in 1956.

Hank Greenberg was born New Year's Day in New York City. He grew up in the Bronx, playing baseball. But when the opportunity came for him to join his hometown team, the New York Yankees, he turned them down and went to Detroit instead. The way Hank Greenberg saw it, the Yankees had the incredible Lou Gehrig at first base. He was ready to play right away.

Taking the League by Storm

Hank Greenberg's first eight seasons, all over .300, had some phenomenal highlights. In his second year he led the league with 63 doubles. In his third he was at the top in home runs and RBIs. In 1937, his fifth year, he totaled 183 RBIs, one short of Lou Gehrig's record. In 1938 he belted 58 home runs, again leading the league. Greenberg lost four and a half years during his prime to war. But he returned in 1945 to lead the Tigers to a pennant.

CAREER STATISTICS	
Batting average	.313
At bats	5,193
Hits	1,828
Doubles	379
Triples	71
Home runs	331
Runs scored	1,051
Runs batted in	1,276
Walks	852

Ken Griffey Jr.

PLAYED 1989–PRESENT

George Kenneth Griffey Jr. is the Seattle Mariners center fielder and one of the top players in the game today. In his nine-year career, he's had five seasons with 100 RBIs or more, four seasons with 40 or more home runs, and seven seasons with a .300 average or better.

Just Like Dad

With a father who was as dominant in sports as Ken Griffey Sr. was, it was inevitable that Junior should head in that direction, too. The extent to which he has succeeded, though, is far beyond anyone's wildest expectations. He is the seventh youngest major league player to reach 200 home runs and the sixth youngest ever to get 1,000 hits. The players in front of him are all in the Hall of Fame. If he would just stop breaking bones in his wrists and hands, and if the players and owners wouldn't stop more seasons, who knows how far he'll go.

Junior was the Mariners' first overall pick in the 1987 draft. He's been with them ever since. He's Seattle's all-time hit leader. He's the first Mariner with 100 steals and 100 homers. The list goes on, since he holds the lead position in most other categories, too.

A Volcano Waiting to Erupt

He began his major league career in 1989 after finishing spring training with a .359 batting average, two home runs, and 21 RBIs. The Mariners weren't disappointed that they put him on the major league roster when Junior hit a home run off of the first pitch he saw in the Seattle Kingdome. But the end of his first year came in July when he broke a bone in his finger.

In 1991 he had a phenomenal season and set a few new Mariner records. His average was .327, he hit 42 doubles, and clubbed three grand slam home runs, all new records. He also hit 22 homers and 100 RBIs that year. In 1992 he hit .308, with 27 homers and 103 RBIs.

In July 1993 he started to hit a home run in every game. By the time he reached six games in a row, people were wondering if he could break the major league record of eight in a row. Number seven was a grand slam against Minnesota. Number eight, again against Minnesota, reached the third deck. In his ninth game, however, his streak was broken, but just barely. He went 2-for-4, and one of his hits was a double that hit the wall. He tied a record with Don Mattingly and Dale Long by hitting at least one home run in eight consecutive games.

The junior and senior Griffeys were the first father and son combination ever to both be playing in the majors. Seattle signed them both. On August 31, 1990, Junior and his father hit back-to-back home runs. When Junior hit a home run in the 1992 All-Star game and was voted the MVP, he and his father became the only father-son duo to accomplish that, since Ken Griffey Sr. did it in 1980.

The Kid Keeps Coming Back

In 1994 he lost out on a chance for a record-breaking season because of the strike. When the season ended early, he had 40 home runs and was batting .323, with 140 hits. His hopes were dashed again in 1995. In May he was heading back to the wall in right-center field to catch a fly ball. He leapt and crashed into the wall. He made the out, but he broke both the bones in his left wrist. The surgery the next day put a plate and seven screws into his wrist to hold it together.

In 1996 he launched 49 dingers and 140 runs, even though he missed a month during the season. He came back in 1997 and took another run at the home run records. He finished with 56 homers to lead the AL.

CAREER STATISTICS

Batting average	.302
At bats	4,593
Hits	1,389
Doubles	261
Triples	24
Home runs	294
Runs scored	820
Runs batted in	872
Walks	580

Tony Gwynn

Anthony Keith Gwynn is the San Diego Padres right fielder. He leads all current players in career batting average with .340. He's had 15 straight seasons over .300, the longest in the majors, and the last five have been over .350. If he were to stop now, he'd be 16th on the all-time batting-average list.

Baseball's Purest Hitter

If he continues his torrid hitting pace, Tony Gwynn is a shoe-in for the 3,000 hit club. At the start of the 1998 season, he is 220 hits short. For Gwynn, that may only be a season away. He's had five 200+ hit seasons, and he would have had a sixth had the 1994 strike not gotten in the way.

That year was devastating to Gwynn. Not only did he manage to notch 165 hits in the shortened season, but he was hitting .394 when the season ended. He was the game's best hope since Ted Williams for breaking the .400 mark. The last time someone in the NL reached that milestone was Bill Terry in 1930.

A Student at the Plate

Gwynn's astonishing ability at the plate is no accident. He works hard to improve and knows every tiny millimeter of his swing. The videotape is his best batting coach. After every game, he replays his turns at the plate, analyzing what he did right and what he did wrong. It's an incredibly helpful tool for him.

Tony Gwynn's videotaping has become legendary, but it started almost by accident. During a slump in 1983, he asked his wife to tape a game on TV so he could see his swing. After the game, when he looked at the tape, Tony knew exactly what was wrong. "I saw right away what I was doing. I couldn't wait to get to the ballpark and correct it. Took me 15 swings. Hit .333 the rest of the year."

After that, the videotape became almost an obsession. He watches after every game and sometimes during a game. He makes copies of the tape and then edits out the rest of the game, so he just has his at bats. He'll then put the good at bats on different tapes, depending on what type of hit he got. He then studies these tapes in the off-season. He doesn't save his bad at bats. Once he's analyzed them and corrected his flaws they're history. He doesn't want to get a bad image in his mind. The process obviously works. His streak of five years batting over .350, which still can continue, ties him at number three on the all-time list. Only Ty Cobb and Rogers Hornsby are ahead of him. (Al Simmons also hit over .350 for five straight seasons.)

Tony Gwynn looks at the videotape of his performance every night after the game. Sometimes that's too late for him. If he's not performing well during a game, he will race back to the clubhouse between innings and watch the replays of his at bats. Occasionally, he can catch something wrong with his swing and fix it to save his plate performance.

Hits Over Glory

Despite his incredible batting average, Tony Gwynn has never won an MVP award. The power hitters get the glory. Like Ty Cobb, Gwynn respects the base hit and high average more than the home run, but he's starting to understand that most other people think differently. "Took me a long time to grasp it. I mean, I hit .370 in 1987, and I finished eighth in the MVP voting. I couldn't understand that then. Last year I hit .394, and I finished seventh. I'm getting the picture, but it annoyed me for a long time."

Unlike Cobb, Tony Gwynn is not about to sit out a batting race just to protect his title. He is more of the Ted Williams variety player. In his words, "You can't win the batting title that way. You just can't."

Playing Through the Pain

This became an issue in the 1991 batting race. Tony Gwynn had an excellent chance at earning his fifth crown. He was leading the league with a .337 average. But his knee was falling apart, and there was little doubt that he was going to need surgery. His father, among others, urged him to stop playing and get the operation before the end of the season. It was unlikely anyone would match his .337 mark. If he stopped then, he was essentially guaranteed the batting title. If he continued to play, then his hurting knee would probably ruin his average. Tony played, because in his mind it wouldn't have been fair to quit. The knee ruined his average. He ended the season at .317.

But there were other years. Tony has now won the batting for four straight seasons (1994–1997). The eight crowns put him in a tie for second on the all-time list with Honus Wagner. Only Ty Cobb, who has 12, is ahead of Gwynn. But Tony still has some good years left in him. He seems to get better with age.

Blue-collar Hitter

Gwynn has worked hard to become a great hitter, but he keeps his approach simple and basic. He uses the entire field when he hits, which makes him difficult to defend. Gwynn hits the ball where it's pitched and waits as long as possible before he starts his swing. This keeps him from getting fooled in pitches.

To keeps his swing simple, Gwynn starts from a basic stance with very little movement. Hitters today often have strange-looking stances such as Jay Buhner, or have a lot of movement with the bat like Gary Sheffield. Gwynn just takes a wide stance, and quietly waits to start his swing. He often has a good idea of what and where the pitcher will be throwing. Tony studies each pitcher before he faces him. He analyzes what the pitcher's tendencies are and how he threw against him the previous times he's faced him. When you combine all this preparation with a good eye and a great swing, it's obvious why Tony Gwynn is such a great hitter.

San Diego is grateful to have a guy like Tony Gwynn. He may be the most loyal player in all of baseball. He grew up in San Diego, played college ball at

Despite his size (Gwynn is 5' 11" and 215 pounds), Tony Gwynn uses a relatively small bat. It's a 33-inch, 30½-ounce Louisville Slugger. He is so in touch with his swing and his bat that when a shipment of 30½-ounce bats and 31-ounce bats came in a box together, he could easily tell which was which.

San Diego State University, and has played his entire career with the Padres.

Just when baseball fans thought Gwynn couldn't get any better, he turned in a season like he had in 1997. Gwynn's batting average was outstanding as usual (.372), but for the first time in his career, he decided to hit with some power. He smacked 17 homers and drove in 119 runs. Gwynn is truly an amazing hitter who keeps getting better.

CAREER STATISTICS

Batting average	.340
At bats	8,187
Hits	2,780
Doubles	460
Triples	84
Home runs	107
Runs scored	1,237
Runs batted in	973
Walks	707

Rickey Henderson

PLAYED 1979-PRESENT

Rickey Henley Henderson plays outfield for the Anaheim Angels. He is the all-time leader in stolen bases, with 1,186, and still going. He's already 248 bases ahead of the next player, the retired Lou Brock. He's also fifth on the all-time walk list and seventh on the all-time runs list.

Born to Run

Santa Claus gave Rickey Henderson the gift of speed when he was born on Christmas Day in 1958. In 1991 Rickey became the Man of Steal, baseball's all-time stolen base superman, when he swiped base number 939 to break Lou Brock's major league record. In 1982 he had broken Brock's other record of 118 single-season steals by stealing 130. He has led the league in stolen bases eleven times, another record. He has stolen at least 50 bases in 12 different seasons.

But stealing bases is only part of the baseball superman Rickey Henderson. He needs to get on base, or his stealing ability means nothing. Rickey has no problem with that. He's probably the best leadoff hitter the game has ever seen. He's had six seasons where he's batted over .300. He's led the league twice in walks, drawing over 100 in a season four times in his career. With 1,772, he's number seven on the all-time walk list. The six in front of him made it to the Hall of Fame long ago. It doesn't matter how, but Henderson always seems to find a way to get on base.

On the Move

Henderson bounced around to different teams throughout his career. It seems as if everyone wants him at the top of their lineup. After six years in Oakland, Henderson signed on as a free agent with the Yankees. He then went back to Oakland, where he won his first championship ring. Since then, he's been with Toronto, Oakland (again), San Diego, and Anaheim.

A Burst of Power

Rickey also hits for power. Seventy times he has started a game with a leadoff home run. He's far and away the all-time leader in that category. And leadoff home runs are more valuable than just one run. On top of the immediate lead it gives to his team, the psychological benefit (and damage if you're the other team) can't be measured. And Rickey hasn't stopped at his first at bat of the game. He's hit 244 home runs in his career. Home runs seem to be the only thing that can stop Rickey from stealing bases.

Even though Rickey Henderson hit just .241 in 1996, his on-base percentage was a whopping .410. The only players in the NL who were ahead of him in that category were Gary Sheffield, Barry Bonds, Jeff Bagwell, and Mike Piazza.

Even at 36, when his speed has slowed and his steals have dropped to match his age, Rickey is still a powerful leadoff hitter. His on-base percentage in 1996 was the fifth-best in the NL, and once again he topped 100 runs. Even after 18 years in the majors, Rickey is still running smoothly.

Henderson has been a part of several winning teams. He was the leadoff hitter for the Oakland As when they went to the World Series three consecutive years from 1988 to 1990. He also led off for the Toronto Blue Jays when they captured the World Series title in 1993. Chances are, when Rickey Henderson is at the top of your lineup, your team has a good shot at winning.

CAREER STATISTICS

Batting average	.286
At bats	8,931
Hits	2,550
Doubles	426
Triples	59
Home runs	252
Runs scored	1,913
Runs batted in	921
Walks	1,772

Rogers Hornsby

Rogers "Rajah" Hornsby had 19 years over .300, four years over .400, and he topped the charts in nearly every category at least once. He won the Triple Crown twice. He is considered the greatest right-handed hitter ever to play the game and was inducted into the Hall of Fame in 1942.

A Clone to Cobb

Although he is second overall to Ty Cobb, Rogers Hornsby holds the top spot for lifetime batting average in the NL. Cobb hit .367. Hornsby hit .358. Hornsby is also second to Cobb in another category. He was the second-most-disliked player ever to grace the game. Like Cobb, Hornsby's bad attitude stemmed from a love of the game and a drive to excel. Since so much of their mind had to be focused on the game, little was left to please the public. But their attention to the game had to be admired. Rogers once said, "People ask me what I do in winter when there's no baseball. I'll tell you what I do. I stare out the window and wait for spring."

Rogers Hornsby was born in Winters, Texas, on April 27, 1896. His mother named him Rogers because that was her maiden name. His older brother, also a ball player, got him a tryout with the Dallas team. They sent him to Oklahoma. In 1915 he was back in Texas, but by the end of the season he had signed on with the St. Louis Cardinals. That first year he only hit .246. The next year he broke .300, and his average hovered around that mark until 1920.

Double Impact

In 1920 two things happened. First, Hornsby was moved from shortstop to second base. Second, he found his stroke. He won the batting title for the next six years, with his 1920's average of .370 being his lowest for the run.

If any one player had a major influence on Hornsby's hitting, it was probably Babe Ruth. Though Ruth probably never gave Hornsby hitting advice, he may have changed Hornsby's approach at the plate by hitting the long ball.

Ruth burst onto the scene as a hitter in 1919, when he hit 29 homers for the Red Sox. That same year, Hornsby hit eight dingers. The Yankees paid Ruth an enormous amount of money to hit homers in New York. He hit 59, Hornsby hit nine. But Rogers seemed to catch on from that point on. He smacked 21 in 1921, and then 42 a year later.

Some people complained that Hornsby was like ice; cold and unfeeling. There's enough evidence to indicate they might be right. When his mother died, Hornsby postponed her funeral until after the World Series. It didn't distract him a bit. He and the Cardinals went on to beat the Yankees in seven games. And when his son died in a plane crash, his first comment was "I told that kid that if he kept going up in those things he'd come down in one the hard way someday."

Obsessed with the Game

Hornsby was always the first player at the ballpark. He could talk baseball to anyone forever, but he had little interest in talking to anyone about anything else. Later, when he was a manager, he even gave batting tips to players on the team he was about to play. He loved baseball and figured if one player improved, the entire game improved.

He could never accept that other players didn't have the same devotion to the game that he had. When he was manager, he wouldn't allow anything but baseball in the clubhouse. No one could smoke, drink a soda, or even read the newspaper. But his obsessive nature didn't work for him as a manager. The players resented him as much as he resented them.

As a hitter, however, all his single-mindedness paid off. He won the batting crown seven times in his career, with every single one of those crowns earned with an average over .370. In 1924 he had a single season average of .424, the highest of the 20th century. He had seven 200-hit seasons, leading the league four times. He totaled ten seasons with home runs in the double digits.

The Best of the Best

But it was a string of five years, from 1921 through 1925, that truly made Hornsby famous. He is the only player ever to average over .400 in a five-year span. But to top it off, he didn't just hit for average. His home run total during those years averaged close to 30. In 1922 and 1925, he won the Triple Crown. Both of those seasons his average was over .400, and his home run totals were 42 and 39, respectively. The season in 1922 made him the only player ever to hit over .400 and slug over 40 home runs.

Hornsby had crazy theories about what would hurt his hitting. He never went to the movies, read a book, or even read a newspaper because he thought it would weaken his eyes.

In 1924, when he hit .424, he also led the league in walks, with 89 of them. Pitchers were scared to put the ball anywhere near the plate, afraid of what he might do to it. When his hits and walks are added together, he was on base more than half the time he was up to bat!

Feared with the Stick

Even though pitchers were scared of Hornsby's hitting, he did not scare them as a person, the way Ty Cobb or Al Simmons had. He was described more like ice at the plate, rather than fire. If he was brushed back by a pitch, he didn't charge the mound, he merely stood back up and resumed his batting stance and icy stare. A writer once asked him if there was a pitcher he feared. He responded that he just felt sorry for them.

Hornsby hit in 33 consecutive games and set a NL record. There are a lot of theories about why Hornsby was such a good hitter, and there's probably some truth to all of them. To begin with, there was his drive. He had it in his mind to succeed, and there was no room for failure. Second, he had a very smooth, technically correct stroke with a beautiful follow through. And, finally, he had a good eye. He simply did not hit the bad pitches. He felt that was key. When he was a batting coach, he imparted a sound piece of advice to a young Ted Williams, who followed the tip religiously. Hornsby advised Williams

to just "get a good ball to hit." Williams stuck with that approach throughout his entire career.

Hornsby had a unique career in that he was a player-manager for more than half of it. He had double duties in St. Louis in 1925 and 1926 and also with the New York Giants in 1927 and the Boston Braves in 1928. He became player-manager in Chicago in 1930 and returned to St. Louis in 1934. He stayed on the player roster for 23 years, but only played in 56 games the last four years of his career.

CAREER STATISTICS	
Batting average	.358
At bats	8,173
Hits	2,930
Doubles	541
Triples	169
Home runs	301
Runs scored	1,579
Runs batted in	1,584
Walks	1,038

Joe Jackson

"Shoeless Joe" Jackson is probably considered baseball's biggest loss from the 1919 Black Sox Scandal. In his shortened career, he hit over .300 for 11 straight years, hitting .408 once. His career average is .356, putting him third on the all-time list.*

Joe Jackson is an important figure in baseball history for two reasons. First he is considered one of the purest baseball hitters that ever played the game. Babe Ruth tried to copy his swing, and even Ty Cobb admired the way Jackson swung the bat. But he also will be remembered as the best of the eight infamous Chicago White Sox players who fixed the 1919 World Series.

Crime Doesn't Pay

For a total of $100,000, eight Chicago White Sox players played so that the Cincinnati Reds would win the series and some big time gamblers would make a lot of money. While there's no disputing the fact that Jackson knew about the plot, his performance in the games shows that he in no way went along with it. He batted .375 for the series and didn't make a single error.

A left-handed hitter with a sweet swing, Jackson could hit for power as well as average. His numbers would have improved if he continued to play after the Dead Ball Era (1920).

CAREER STATISTICS

Batting average	.356
At bats	4,981
Hits	1,774
Doubles	307
Triples	168
Home runs	54
Runs scored	873
Runs batted in	785
Walks	519

Reggie Jackson

PLAYED 1967-1987

*R*eginald Martinez "Mr. October" Jackson is sixth on the all-time list of home run leaders. He played in five World Series with a .357 average, putting him ninth on the all-time list. He tops the chart in World Series slugging average, is fifth in home runs, and eighth in RBIs.

Reggie Jackson was born in Wyncote, Pennsylvania, in 1946. His father had been a player in the Negro Leagues. In high school it looked as though Reggie might use his athletic talents elsewhere. Even though Jackson was an outstanding baseball star, it was football that brought him all the attention. He was given an amazing 51 scholarship offers from various colleges.

The Birth of a Star

Jackson chose Arizona State and played both football and baseball. All of a sudden, he was being noticed for his baseball. The Kansas City Athletics grabbed him. A year after Reggie hit the big time, in 1968, the team moved to Oakland. Although Reggie led the league in strikeouts that year (and for the next three), he did hit 29 home runs. But the move to Oakland was good for him. In 1969 his career began to take off.

He hit 47 home runs that year. Remarkably, he didn't lead the league in homers, but he did top the charts in slugging average and runs. For 16 of his 21 years playing, he hit over 20 home runs, and many of those years he hit over 30 and 40. He is sixth on the all-time home run list, with a total of 563. Of course, he's first on the strike-out list.

How Sweet It Is

In 1976 Reggie was traded to Baltimore, and then a year later to the New York Yankees. New York was made for Reggie Jackson. He once said, "If I ever played in New York, they'd name a candy bar after me." They did.

Reggie loved playing in front of the wild crowds and loved talking to the press. He became a personality as well as a player, and the fans either loved or hated him. His teammates felt the same way. They loved him in October, but his bragging to the media bothered them. He called himself "the straw that stirs the drink," which his teammates were not too fond of.

Reggie Jackson produced one of the greatest individual performances in World Series history. During the 1977 World Series, he hit three home runs in one game on three consecutive swings. Each was on the first pitch and hit off of a different pitcher.

Show Time

But Reggie helped the team in other ways. He led the Yankees to two World Series championships, in 1977 and 1978. In the 1977 series, he batted .450 and hit five home runs, and in 1978, he hit .397 and slugged two home runs. Mr. October knew where the spotlight was. The series was the biggest show in baseball, so baseball's biggest performer had to turn it on. But he earned every bit of the attention he got.

When he finally retired in 1987, it was an agonizing decision for him. He had 563 home runs. If he retired then, he was sixth on the all-time list. If he stuck it out, playing one more year, he could probably hit 11 more home runs, beating out Harmon Killebrew for the fifth spot on the list. He'd never hit less than 14 in a season, so it was a good gamble. Reggie knew how to play the crowds. He made his debate public and captured the fans attention once again. Everyone was wondering. In the end, Reggie Jackson decided to retire.

CAREER STATISTICS	
Batting average	.262
At bats	9,864
Hits	2,584
Doubles	463
Triples	49
Home runs	563
Runs scored	1,551
Runs batted in	1,702
Walks	1,375

Chipper Jones

*L*arry "Chipper" Jones Jr. is the Atlanta Braves third baseman and shortstop. He's hit double-digit home runs in his full three years in the majors, and his average in 1996 was .309.

A Teacher and His Son

Chipper Jones grew up in Pierson, Florida, the only child of Lynn and Larry Jones. Larry Sr. is a teacher and baseball coach who once had a tryout for the Cubs. Right from the start, he showed his son the beauty of baseball.

They had a hay barn in their backyard, and Chipper and his father used to play a game between the house and the barn. They would throw a tennis ball and try to strike each other out. By the time Chipper was 13, his father couldn't beat him. Then Chipper decided to be a switch-hitter. They'd play the same game, and Chipper would pretend to be a major league team's lineup. He'd switch sides, depending on who was up at bat.

Let the Kid Play

Chipper Jones was the top draft choice in the 1990 draft. The pitcher Todd Van Poppel was actually the Braves first pick, but he had said he would only play for Oakland. The Braves decided not to test his statement and went for Chipper Jones. When the Braves made an offer, Larry Jones felt it was much too low. He wanted to hold out. Chipper wanted to play. He told his father to split the difference with the Braves. He said, "I'm going to make my money in the big leagues, not off this deal right here." He signed for $350,000, and two weeks later he was playing rookie league baseball. (Todd Van Poppel signed for $1.2 million and has struggled in the majors.)

Chipper's performance in the minors was outstanding—he was hitting .330 and clubbing double-digit home runs. But during spring training in 1994, he tore the ligaments in his left knee, avoiding a tag at first base. He lost an entire summer.

A Blue-Chipper

His first year stats brought him close to the Rookie of the Year award. He hit .265, with 23 home runs and 86 RBIs. Four times in the 1995 season he had four-hit games, and three times he won the game for the Braves with ninth-inning home runs. On top of that, he was a standout in postseason play, as the Braves became the world champions. Chipper hit .364, with three home runs and eight RBIs.

The next year Chipper Jones continued to impress. He batted .309, belted 30 home runs, and brought in 110 RBIs. In 1997 he finished at .295, with 21 homers and 111 RBIs. The Braves have signed him through the year 2000.

The nickname "Chipper" comes from "chip off the old block," and Chipper truly is just like his father. His mother claims they are "absolute clones. They stand the same way, they walk the same, they field the same."

Chipper likes his nickname. "If I was called Larry Jones, who'd remember that? Chipper is one of those first names people remember. Think of Cal, Emmitt, Mickey. You hear those names, and you say, 'Those were some of the best to ever play the game.' I'd like to be thought of like that someday."

CAREER STATISTICS

Batting average	.291
At bats	1,219
Hits	500
Doubles	95
Triples	11
Home runs	74
Runs scored	301
Runs batted in	307
Walks	236

Al Kaline

Albert William Kaline retired with 3,007 hits and a batting average of .297. During his 22-year career, he also managed to hit 399 home runs. He was inducted into the Hall of Fame in 1980.

Al Kaline was born into a baseball family. His grandfather, his father, and all of his uncles played semipro ball. Al was destined to make a career out of it. When he graduated high school, he was signed by the Detroit Tigers.

A Star in His Teens

He was only 18, but Kaline went straight to the majors, never playing a single game in the minor leagues. His first year, 1953, he played in only 30 games, but after that he became the Tigers' regular outfielder. In 1955 he took the batting title with a .340 average and led the league in hits with exactly 200. He also socked 27 home runs. He was only 20-years-old and the youngest player ever to win the batting title.

Al finally got a chance to play in the World Series in 1968. He hit .379 with two home runs as the Tigers won the title in seven games. He drove in eight runs while scoring six and had a game-winning, bases-loaded single in the seventh inning of game five. The Tigers came back after losing three of the first four games.

CAREER STATISTICS

Batting average	.297
At bats	10,116
Hits	3,007
Doubles	498
Triples	75
Home runs	399
Runs scored	1,622
Runs batted in	1,583
Walks	1,277

Wee Willie Keeler

Willie "Wee Willie" Keeler will always be remem-bered for his batting advice: "Keep your eyes clear, and hit 'em where they ain't." His lifetime batting average was .343. Most impressive, though, is his 44-game hitting streak, which he set in 1897. This record lasted until Joe DiMaggio broke it in 1941. Willie Keeler was inducted into the Hall of Fame in 1939.

Big Things Come in Small Packages

At 5'4" and 120 pounds, Wee Willie Keeler just went for base hits. He had the advantage of playing baseball in a time where the rules were slightly different. Foul balls were not counted as strikes. He could deliberately foul ball after ball, even by bunting them foul, until he got a pitch he liked.

Keeler was considered a nice guy playing with a bunch of bullies (although the fans loved the bullies, too). During his peak years, 1894-1898 (he won the batting title in 1897 and 1898), he played for the Baltimore Orioles. They won the pennant three years in a row, coming in second the next two.

Keeler played his last four seasons with the New York Highlanders. He retired with a lifetime average of .343, and was eighth on the all-time list.

CAREER STATISTICS	
Batting average	.343
At bats	8,585
Hits	2,947
Doubles	237
Triples	150
Home runs	34
Runs scored	1,727
Runs batted in	810
Walks	524

Harmon Killebrew

Harmon Clayton "Killer" Killebrew had eight seasons where he hit over 40 home runs. He led the league in home runs six times; in RBIs three times. With 573 home runs in his career, he is fifth on the all-time list. He was inducted into the Hall of Fame in 1984.

When Harmon Killebrew was in high school in Idaho, he was so much better than anyone he was playing against that his batting average was .847, and half of his hits were home runs. He was Idaho's darling, and a state senator even got into the act when it was time for Harmon to look at a major league career. A scout came out to watch, and Harmon didn't let the senator down. He blasted a 435-foot homer. He was signed immediately.

A Test of Patience

His career started slowly. Professional baseball had added a new rule called the "bonus rule." It basically said that a player who signed for more than $4,000 had to be kept on the major league roster for two years, even if he was playing in the minor leagues. Because Killebrew was a "bonus" player, he didn't see much action in his first couple of years. In fact, he played a total of 47 games. Then for the next three years, he was sent to the minors, with occasional major league appearances. Finally, in 1959 he had his first full season.

He was playing for the Washington Senators, and the fans must have wondered where this young man had been for the past five years. He slugged his way to the top in this rookie year, leading the league in home runs with 42 of them. For four of the next five seasons, he also socked over 40 homers.

A Killer Swing

Harmon Killebrew didn't hit for average, but he sure had the power. He is behind only Babe Ruth on the AL home run chart. For 14 straight seasons, he hit over 20 home runs, and in eight of those seasons, he hit more than 40. But at the same time, he never hit over .300 and ranks tenth overall on the strikeout list. He sacrificed his batting average to take big cuts at the ball. He could draw a walk, however, topping the charts in that category four times. One of those years, 1969, he led in walks, home runs, on-base percentage, and RBIs. He was voted the year's MVP.

Harmon Killebrew was in the lineup to hit home runs and nothing else. In 8,147 at bats, Killebrew did not have one sacrifice bunt in his career. He was also the first home run champion whose batting average was below .250.

Killebrew was given the nickname "Killer" because he tried to murder the ball every time he swung the bat. He never got cheated on a swing, putting his entire body into it. Even though he struck out 1,699 times, Killebrew will be better remembered for his long, towering home runs that left pitchers in a daze.

The Washington Senators never even won a division title, but when the team moved to Minnesota and became the Twins, they did a little better. They won the division title three times and the pennant once. In 1965 they lost their bid for the championship in seven games. That was Harmon Killebrew's only trip to the World Series. He did manage to notch six hits, including a solo home run off Dodger pitcher Don Drysdale.

CAREER STATISTICS

Batting average	.256
At bats	8,147
Hits	2,086
Doubles	290
Triples	24
Home runs	573
Runs scored	1,283
Runs batted in	1,584
Walks	1,559

Ralph Kiner

 PLAYED 1946–1955

Ralph McPherran Kiner lost his early playing years to World War II, but he made up for lost time when he came back. In his first seven years in the majors, he led the league in home runs and home run percentage. He's second on the all-time list in home run percentage. He was inducted into the Hall of Fame in 1975.

Ralph Kiner homered once every 14 times he came to bat. Only Babe Ruth has been able to do better than that. His all-time home run total was 369. That's impressive, but it's even more amazing that he was able to get so many when he only played for ten years. But home runs were his goal every time he came to bat. As he put it, "Players who hit for average drive Fords. Players who hit for home runs drive Cadillacs."

Instant Power

Kiner played his first seven years with the Pittsburgh Pirates and led the league in home runs and home run percentage every single one of those years. He hit over 50 homers twice and over 40 three times. He played a little more than seven years with the Pittsburgh Pirates and finished his career with the Chicago Cubs and the St. Louis Cardinals. During his years with the Pirates, fans named the left-field corner at Forbes Field "Kiner's Korner."

CAREER STATISTICS	
Batting average	.279
At bats	5,205
Hits	1,451
Doubles	216
Triples	39
Home runs	369
Runs scored	971
Runs batted in	1,015
Walks	1,011

Chuck Klein

Charles Herbert Klein was a Phillies slugger who could also hit for average. He topped the charts in home runs four straight years and captured the Triple Crown in 1933. He retired with a .320 lifetime average.

Chuck Klein had a phenomenal start. In each of his first five full seasons, he hit well over .300, gathered over 200 hits, clubbed over 25 home runs (in four of the five he hit over 30), and knocked in over 100 RBIs.

Philly's Basher

In 1929, Chuck Klein's second year in the big leagues, he set the NL record for most homers hit in a season. He belted 43 that year, which was one more than Rogers Hornsby's record set in 1922. Unfortunately, Chuck's record was not on the books long. One year later, Hack Wilson clubbed 56.

Even though Klein won the Triple Crown in 1933 with a .368 batting average, 28 home runs, and 120 RBIs, his numbers were better three years earlier. That year he hit .386, 40 home runs, and 170 RBIs. He also had 250 hits. Klein was traded to the Cubs in 1934, and his career took a nosedive. He went back to the Phillies in 1936, and he became one of the few players ever to slug four home runs in one game. He entered the Hall of Fame in 1980.

CAREER STATISTICS

Batting average	.320
At bats	6,486
Hits	2,076
Doubles	398
Triples	74
Home runs	300
Runs scored	1,168
Runs batted in	1,202
Walks	601

Napoleon Lajoie

Napoleon "Nap" Lajoie was one of the first stars of the AL. In his first year he won the triple crown, batting .422 with 14 home runs and 125 RBIs. His .422 in 1901 set an AL record for season average that still stands. He was elected to the Hall of Fame in 1936.

In 1896 Napoleon Lajoie began his major league career in the NL, playing second base for the Philadelphia Phillies. He switched to the higher-paying AL in 1901 and won the Triple Crown in his first season.

He also became the biggest star of the new league playing for the Philadelphia Athletics. When Ty Cobb entered the league, the two battled for the batting title frequently. One season it almost got them banned from baseball.

A Heated Battle

In 1910 the two of them were in hot contention for the season's batting title. Everyone wanted Cobb to lose. Ahead by a few points, Cobb sat out the final game of the season. Lajoie had a double header, and the infield on the opposing team decided to help Lajoie. He dropped down six bunt hits to win the title. But the league found out about the scam and stripped Lajoie of the crown. He retired with 3,244 career hits.

CAREER STATISTICS

Batting average	.338
At bats	9,592
Hits	3,244
Doubles	658
Triples	161
Home runs	83
Runs scored	1,503
Runs batted in	1,599
Walks	516

Barry Larkin

Barry Louis Larkin is the Cincinnati Reds shortstop. When he won the MVP award in 1995, he was the first NL shortstop since 1962 to receive that award. He is also the first shortstop in history to reach the elite 30-30 mark. In 1996 he hit 33 home runs and stole 36 bases.

A Budding Star

Barry Larkin was earning honors in baseball well before he ever became a pro. He was All-American in college and the first player ever to win the MVP in the Big Ten conference two years in a row. Instead of going straight to the pros, Barry opted to join the 1984 Olympic Team. The team won the silver medal, and then it was time for Barry to go pro.

The Cincinnati Reds selected him in their first round, the fourth pick in the draft in 1985, and by August of 1986, Larkin was in the majors. By 1988 he was one of their top hitters. That year, except for once, he never went hitless two games in a row. He ended the season with a 21-game hitting streak, which was the longest in the league that year. He also struck out fewer times than any other major leaguer, with a mere 24 strikeouts during the whole season.

Return to Glory

The next year Larkin was hitting .342 when he badly injured his elbow making a throw. He lost the rest of the year, but came back strong in 1990 to earn the Reds' MVP Award. He had four hitting streaks that season of ten or more games. The Reds won the World Series that year, and Larkin's series average of .353 was a large part of the reason why.

In 1991 he decided he wanted to give something back to the Cincinnati community. He started "the Caring Team," an organization to help children's charities. It caught on and is now national. The charities get money each time a Caring Team athlete gets a hit. Larkin received the Roberto Clemente Award for his efforts.

He won the MVP award in 1995, with a batting average of .319, 15 homers, and 51 stolen bases. Despite those numbers, the vote was controversial, with many people thinking they weren't quite at the MVP level. Many of Larkin's detractors thought that Dante Bichette deserved the award, since his average and home run and RBI totals were all higher.

Barry Larkin played shortstop for the 1984 U.S. Olympic baseball team. His teammates included Mark McGwire, Jim Abbott, and Will Clark.

Making It Happen

But 1995 was a vote for the intangibles. Like Kenny Lofton and Rickey Henderson, Barry Larkin made good things happen for the team whenever he got on base. On top of that, his fielding was excellent. The Reds, Barry Larkin, and many others felt it was nice to have consistency and leadership recognized for the valuable asset that it is. Hall of Famer Hank Aaron agrees when he says, "I can't think of anybody who is doing what Barry Larkin is doing combination-wise."

Larkin battled nagging injuries in 1996, but had another solid season. He batted .296 and hit a career-high 33 homers. His 1997 season was cut short by an ankle injury despite hitting .317 in 224 at bats. Hopefully, Larkin can keep his health in the future and return to his former MVP status.

CAREER STATISTICS	
Batting average	.299
At bats	5,770
Hits	1,547
Doubles	271
Triples	51
Home runs	139
Runs scored	862
Runs batted in	646
Walks	592

Kenny Lofton

Kenneth Lofton is the leadoff hitter and center fielder for the Atlanta Braves. With his high average and phenomenal base-stealing ability, he makes things happen on the base paths. He's hit over .300 the last four years of his five-year career, leading the league in steals every year.

Against All Odds

Kenny Lofton was born on May 31, 1967, in a bad neighborhood in East Chicago, Indiana. His mother was only 14 when she had him, and while she went back to school, Kenny was raised by his grandmother. He never knew his father. Kenny's family didn't have much money. His grandfather had died seven years earlier, and they lived only on his social security checks. Kenny's grandmother couldn't work because she was almost blind from glaucoma. Kenny was determined that one day he would make enough money to move his grandmother to a better place. There's no doubt now that Kenny is going to have lots of money for a long time.

He played basketball and baseball in high school, but basketball seemed to be his stronger sport. He was given a full ride to Arizona to play hoops. Just for fun he went out for the baseball team, and a scout for the Houston Astros saw his speed on the base paths. Houston picked him in the 17th round of the draft. He played in the minors, and 20 games in the majors, but he wouldn't get instruction after the season ended because he had promised his grandmother he'd get a college degree. He went back to Arizona to graduate. The Astros traded him to Cleveland.

The Indians put him in the majors immediately. They gave him a crash course in hitting, base stealing, and bunting. He was a fast learner and a hard worker, spending hour after hour in the batting cages. The Indian general manager John Hart said, "He's very coachable, and he was very sincere about improving himself."

Fast Learner, Faster Runner

The Indians knew they had a gem. In his first season, Lofton hit .285 and led the league in steals with 66. He's been at the top of the stolen base list every year since. His second year in the majors, 1993, he hit .325. He hasn't hit below .310 since. He is an outstanding bunter, and with his speed he often gets base hits using that strategy. "I'll do anything to get on base," he said. "And once I get on, a lot of things can happen. If the pitcher's so worried about my baserunning that he ends up not throwing the pitch where he wants to, then he's in trouble. And I'm doing my job."

Kenny is now making several million dollars a year and has given money to his grandmother, but he's also given lots to underprivileged children in East Chicago and Cleveland.

His teammates on the Indians were well aware of what he did for them. When Kenny was hot and got on base, the Indians tended to win. When he didn't, they tended to lose. Cleveland catcher Sandy Alomar said, "Kenny is the spark that ignites our team." And Kevin Seitzer, after he came to the Indians in a trade, said, "He's probably the best leadoff hitter I've ever played with. . . . He has great instincts on the bases, and there's nobody in the game who's as good a bunter."

Right before the start of the 1997 season, Kenny Lofton was traded to the Atlanta Braves. It's a little early to say who got the better end of the deal, but the Braves got themselves one of the game's most exciting players. He hit .333, scoring 90 runs, despite missing over a month of the season with a groin injury. He is, without a doubt, one of the best leadoff hitters of his time.

CAREER STATISTICS

Batting average	.316
At bats	3,314
Hits	1,047
Doubles	153
Triples	48
Home runs	44
Runs scored	641
Runs batted in	309
Walks	371

Bill Madlock

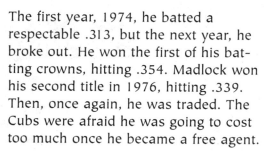

PLAYED 1973–1987

William "Mad Dog" Madlock Jr. played for seven different major league teams in his career. He captured the batting title four times and retired with a lifetime average of .305.

Don't Unpack

Bill Madlock began his career with the Washington Senators in 1969, but he never got to the majors with them. He was traded to Texas and played 21 games with the Rangers in 1973. He did fairly well in limited play, hitting .351, but he was traded to the Cubs.

The first year, 1974, he batted a respectable .313, but the next year, he broke out. He won the first of his batting crowns, hitting .354. Madlock won his second title in 1976, hitting .339. Then, once again, he was traded. The Cubs were afraid he was going to cost too much once he became a free agent.

They traded him to San Francisco. In 1979 the Giants traded him to Pittsburgh in mid season. Madlock hit .328 for them, helping them win the world championship.

He stayed with the Pirates for five more years and then was off to the Dodgers at the end of the 1985 season to help them win the pennant. He finished his career in Detroit, where he hit 17 home runs in his final season. It was the most he hit in his career.

CAREER STATISTICS	
Batting average	.305
At bats	6,594
Hits	2,008
Doubles	348
Triples	34
Home runs	163
Runs scored	920
Runs batted in	860
Walks	605

Mickey Mantle

Mickey Charles Mantle, having played the revered Yankee center fielder position for 16 years, is eighth on the list for all-time home runs. He hit 536, banging dingers in double digits every year of his career. He also had ten years of an average .300 or higher, retiring with a lifetime average of .298. He went to 12 World Series and tops the chart in five of those categories. He was inducted into the Hall of Fame in 1974.

Mickey Mantle was born on October 20, 1931 in Spavinaw, Oklahoma. His father, Elvin "Mutt" Mantle, was a huge baseball fan and named his firstborn son after Mickey Cochrane, the Hall of Fame catcher. (Mickey Mantle always said that he was lucky his father never knew Mickey Cochrane's real name was Gordon Stanley Cochrane.) Mutt Mantle was a lead miner who once played semipro ball. He intended for his son Mickey to achieve everything he couldn't. Mickey spent his childhood playing baseball and being coached by his father. He started switch-hitting as soon as he was swinging the bat. At 16 he was playing for a junior league team when a Yankee scout saw him. He was quickly signed up.

The Passing of the Torch

He started playing right field for the Yankees in 1951, next to Joe DiMaggio, who was in center. DiMaggio was getting on in his years, with hurting heels, but he was still playing. Mickey was young and fast. But when a ball, hit by rookie Willie Mays, came between them in right-center field, DiMaggio called for it. Mickey, in a full sprint, came to a complete stop out of respect for his hero. DiMaggio caught

the ball, but a spike on Mantle's shoe caught the edge of a buried sprinkler head, and his knee snapped. Mickey Mantle went down.

Bandaged and Beaten

That was the first of many injuries to come. It seemed that whenever he took the field, he was taped up somewhere. During his major league career, he broke two bones, destroyed both knees, had an abscessed hip, and a knee cyst and suffered shoulder, elbow, and groin injuries. But remarkably, most of the time, he tried to play through the pain. It will never be known how he might have performed if he weren't constantly having to deal with aches, pains, and sprains. A teammate once said, "If he had been physically sound for even one full season, he would have hit seventy homers."

He did well enough without it. He led the league once in average, four times in home runs, six times in runs, once in triples, and once in RBIs. He went to 12 World Series. In most World Series categories, he's at the top: first in home runs, runs, RBIs, walks, and strikeouts, and second in games, at bats, and hits.

Double Trouble

Mickey was a switch-hitter, who could hit equally as hard on both sides of the plate. It was once said that "right-handed he could hit as

far as Jimmie Foxx, and left-handed he could hit as far as Babe Ruth."
He once crushed a ball out of the Washington Senators' Park. When it
came to rest, a ten-year-old boy picked it. The tape-measure shot
came to 565 feet. When asked if he had ever stepped up to the plate
trying to hit a home run, Mantle responded: "I tried to hit a home run
every time I was up at bat."

In 1956 he had his best year ever,
which happened to be one of the
best years baseball has ever seen.
He won the Triple Crown and MVP
award, slugging 52 home runs,
batting .353, and bringing in 130
runs. He also led the league in runs
with 132 and slugging average with
.705. It was one of the greatest
single seasons a player has had in
the history of baseball.

*Mickey was injury-prone in high
school, too. He had osteomyelitis. He
might have lost a leg and his career might
never have begun if his mother hadn't
gone out of her way to get a brand-new
drug for him: penicillin.*

Chasing a Legend

The year that Roger Maris broke Babe Ruth's home run record, 1961,
was also a big slugging year for Mickey Mantle. In fact, Maris and
Mantle, teammates on the Yankees, seemed to be in a kind of contest.
The media was keeping count, and these two kept slugging away.
Mantle started out with the lead, but then Maris caught up and
passed him. They were neck and neck all summer, but in September,
Mantle was too injured to go on. He stopped that year with 54, and
Maris went on to hit 61.

Enough Is Enough

Mantle continued to hit home runs, but injuries kept him out of the
lineup on a regular basis. In 1962 he appeared in only 123 games.
The following season he played in just 65. In 1964 Mantle had
another outstanding season. He batted .303, with 35 home runs and
111 RBIs. For the rest of his career, he would never hit higher than
.288 or more than 23 homers in a season.

Mickey Mantle retired in 1968 at the age of 36. His injuries and his
hard living had caught up with him. He had played too much both on
and off the field. But he retired with a .298 average and 536 home
runs behind him. He was inducted into the Hall of Fame in 1974. In
the early 1990s, he discovered his hard-drinking days had completely
destroyed his liver. He needed a transplant if he was going to live.

He got one on June 8, 1995. Everyone was optimistic. Mantle himself was a changed man. He went out of his way to publicize his alcohol abuse, hoping to prevent others from following in his footsteps. "Don't be like me," he warned. "God gave me a body and the ability to play baseball. He gave me everything. I just wasted it." Despite everyone's best efforts, however, complications and a weakened body spelled the end. Mickey Mantle died two months after his transplant on August 13, 1995, at the age of 63.

With Mantle's passing went one of America's last sports heroes. Mantle was an icon who captured the imagination of sports fans everywhere. An innocent, Oklahoma farm boy with tremendous talent, "The Mick" will go down as one of the greatest and most well-liked ball players in the history of the game. His humbling final days only endeared him more to the American public.

Mickey Mantle's father, grandfather, and two uncles died from Hodgkin's Disease before they were 40. Mickey was sure he was going to, too. When he was in his mid-forties and still disease-free, he joked, "If I'd known I was going to live this long, I would have taken better care of myself."

CAREER STATISTICS

Batting average	.298
At bats	8,102
Hits	2,415
Doubles	344
Triples	72
Home runs	536
Runs scored	1,677
Runs batted in	1,509
Walks	1,734

Roger Maris

Roger Eugene Maris has the distinction of hitting 61 home runs in a single season of baseball. Nobody in the history of baseball has hit more. The 61st broke Babe Ruth's record, which most people thought was unbeatable. Maris also played in seven World Series in his short 12-year career and earned two MVP awards.

Roger Maris was born in Minnesota but grew up in North Dakota. His high school didn't have a baseball team, so Maris's only chance to play the game was American Legion ball. It was more than enough. He became a star, and the Cleveland Indians found him. He moved on to the Kansas City Athletics and then finally settled in New York, hitting in front of Mickey Mantle. For Maris, it was a great spot. Pitchers weren't going to walk him, because Mantle was on deck. They'd rather take a chance that Maris would get a hit than risk having him on base with Mantle up at bat.

Power in Pinstripes

In his first year with the Yankees, Maris hit 39 home runs and led the league in RBIs with 112. But it was his second year that put him in the record books. He slugged his way through the season, hitting homer after homer. It soon became clear to everyone that finally here was a challenger to Babe Ruth's single-season record of 60.

This news excited some fans but angered others. The somewhat unfriendly Roger Maris had only been there two years. He'd already snagged the MVP award away from Mickey Mantle the year before. It didn't seem right to many that he should be the one to break the

Babe's record. On top of that, the season when Ruth was playing was 154 games long. When Maris was playing, the season had 162 games. When Maris did finally slug number 61 on the last day of the season, the commissioner of baseball insisted that an asterisk be placed next to his name, indicating that the conditions were different. Maris was understandably bitter. The asterisk next to Maris's name was removed in 1991 by commissioner Fay Vincent.

Many of the Yankee fans who were upset that Maris was breaking the Babe's record didn't realize what a team player Maris really was. While he was eager to go for the record, a Yankee win came first. If a third baseman was playing him too deep, Maris would often bunt for a base hit.

Tough Act to Follow

The next year was even tougher for him. He hit 33 home runs, which should have been impressive for anyone, but it seemed that the world was disappointed. Everyone kept after him, asking if he thought he was able to hit more than 61. On top of that, he kept getting injured. Some people accused him of exaggerating his injuries so he'd have an excuse for not hitting more homers. It made him furious. It was almost a relief when he was traded to St. Louis and had to play in the much larger Busch Memorial Stadium. He changed his style and he went for more singles and doubles.

Finally the injuries were too much, and he retired in 1968. But in his short career, Roger Maris had won five pennants with the Yankees and two with St. Louis. He also holds the single-season record for home runs. Yet, he is still not in the Hall of Fame. In 1985 Maris died of cancer at 51.

CAREER STATISTICS

Batting average	.260
At bats	5,101
Hits	1,325
Doubles	195
Triples	42
Home runs	275
Runs scored	826
Runs batted in	850
Walks	652

Edgar Martinez

*E*dgar Martinez is the Seattle Mariner's designated hitter. He has won two AL batting titles and hit above .300 and had double-digit home runs in every full season of his career.

He's the Man

It took a while for Edgar Martinez to cement his position as the Seattle Mariners' third baseman, but once he did, he didn't let them down. They brought him up for partial seasons In 1987, 1988, and 1989. Finally, in 1990, the commitment-shy Mariners gave Edgar a starting spot on Opening Day. He didn't disappoint, batting .302, with 27 doubles.

As solid as those numbers are, when he's played a full season, he's managed to beat them every year since. In 1992 he won his first batting crown and also led the league in doubles with 46. He became only the second player in AL history to win the batting title on a cellar-dwelling, last-place team.

He missed most of 1993 and a large chunk of 1994. He pulled his left hamstring on April 3, 1994, after having team-leading stats in spring training. He rushed his return, and the hamstring never healed. He went back on the disabled list two more times that season for the same injury. The following year he missed the beginning of the season to a bruised right wrist and the end of the season to the strike.

A Clean Bill of Health

But 1995 gave him his second batting crown. He hit .356 and finished third in MVP voting. He led the league in on-base percentage, runs, and doubles. His 29 home runs were a career high. When battling the

Yankees for the AL pennant, he became the first player in history to have seven RBIs in a single postseason game. Three came from a homer in the third inning and four more came from a grand slam in the eighth.

Martinez was also responsible for one of the most exciting moments in Seattle Mariners history. During the 1995 playoffs with the New York Yankees, Martinez came up with the score tied in extra innings in the deciding game of the series. With Ken Griffey Jr. on first base, Martinez lined a double to left field. Griffey raced all the way around the bases to score, and the Mariners advanced to the AL Championship Series.

When Edgar Martinez is mentioned, a player who hits a lot of doubles comes to mind. In 1996 Martinez looked like he would lead the AL in doubles for the third time in five years with 52 of them. But he was bested by his teammate Alex Rodriguez, who totaled 54.

With a repeat 52 doubles in 1996, Edgar Martinez is only the fifth player since 1900 to have consecutive 50-double seasons. He led the Mariners with a .330 batting average in 1997 as they won the AL Western Division for the second time in three years. Martinez also tied Frank Thomas for the highest on-base percentage (.456) in 1997.

CAREER STATISTICS

Batting average	.317
At bats	3,818
Hits	1,210
Doubles	291
Triples	12
Home runs	145
Runs scored	708
Runs batted in	592
Walks	674

Eddie Mathews

Edwin Lee Mathews was the Braves third baseman slugger. He hit 512 home runs in his career and had four seasons where he hit 40 or more. For 14 straight seasons, he hit over 20 home runs, and ten of those were over 30.

Next to the Ruth-and-Gehrig one-two punch, the Aaron-and-Mathews duo is the most famous in baseball. And it actually was more successful than Ruth and Gehrig. Combined, Mathews and Aaron hit more homers than any other pair in the game. It helped that Aaron was right-handed and Mathews was left-handed. In every game, at least one of them had an advantage.

A Nice Dilemma

Mathews grew up in Santa Barbara, California. He played football and baseball in high school and rose to the top in each. The Brooklyn Dodgers and the Boston Braves tried to sign him. He chose the Braves, even though Brooklyn was offering more money. It was a good choice.

His first year in the majors wasn't as impressive as it could have been, as he led the league in strikeouts. But the 25 taters he knocked over the fence showed that there was promise in this young California boy. He proved it the very next year. The franchise moved to Milwaukee, leaving Boston behind. Mathews hit .302 and slugged 47 home runs, winning his first home run title.

Prime Time

For the next nine years, he hit over 30 home runs, reaching the 40 mark three more times. In 1959 he led the league again in homers, and although he also topped the charts in walks four times, he never again was up there for strikeouts.

In 1959 Mathews had one of his most solid seasons at the plate. He hit .306 (only the second time in his career he reached .300), hit 46 home runs, and knocked in 104 runs. Two years later he batted .306 again and stroked 32 homers.

In 1962 Eddie injured his shoulder, and it never fully recovered. While he still put up impressive numbers, his home run total dipped into the twenties. Fortunately, he still led the league in walks, so he could get on base for Hank Aaron to knock him in.

Eddie Mathews and Hank Aaron combined 863 homers as teammates for the Braves. They were also in uniform for the Braves when Aaron broke Babe Ruth's home run record. Only this time, Mathews was Aaron's manager.

Eddie followed the franchise to Atlanta in 1966. But he played there only one year. He tried a year in Houston and a year in Detroit, and then he retired. Although he played in the Braves organization for 15 years, Mathews hit his 500th home run with the Houston Astros in 1967. He helped guide the Tigers to a world championship in 1968. He was inducted into the Hall of Fame in 1978.

CAREER STATISTICS

Batting average	.271
At bats	8,537
Hits	2,315
Doubles	354
Triples	72
Home runs	512
Runs scored	1,509
Runs batted in	1,453
Walks	1,444

Don Mattingly

PLAYED 1982-1995

Donald Arthur Mattingly was the Yankee first baseman. For six straight years, his batting average was over .300; twice it was over .340. In those years he was also hitting double digits in home runs. He had three 200-hit seasons and retired with a lifetime batting average of .307.

Farm Boy Hits the Big City

Evansville, Indiana, the birthplace and current home of Don Mattingly, is a city made up of Mattinglys. The name is like "Smith" in other parts of the country. In Evansville, there are 88 Mattinglys in the phone book, and there are probably some more who, like Don and his family, are unlisted. It's probably one of the reasons Don felt he should keep his family there, despite 15 years of playing baseball for the Yankees in New York. He even opened up a restaurant in Evansville, called Mattinglys' 23. The 23 was his uniform number.

Don was born on April 20, 1961, one of five children and the last of four brothers. He was always being chosen to play wiffle ball with the older kids, so he learned the sport at a young age. As he says, "There's no substitute for learning to play from older brothers." Their backyard was his training ground, and it's easy to see how his hitting style developed. If he pulled the ball, it went into a tree. Left-center was the only place he could get a home run.

A Raise in Salary

At ten Don started making a living off of baseball. He would stand outside the minor league park and pick up the foul balls. These he would sell back to the club for 50 cents apiece. By the end of his career, he was making millions.

Don started off strong his first year in the majors. He only played in 91 games, but he hit .283. It was enough to earn him a full-time position, and the next year, 1983, the Yankees were glad they had him. He hit .343, to win the batting crown. He also led the league in hits with 207, led the league in doubles with 44, and drove in 110 RBIs with 23 home runs.

In 1985 and 1986 the numbers were just as impressive. He led the league in doubles both years, had over 200 hits both years, and hit .324 in 1985 and .352 in 1986. He led the league in RBIs in 1985 and in hits in 1986. Both years he hit over 30 home runs. His 1986 hit total of 238 puts him fifteenth on the all-time list of single-season hits.

Mattingly has always been ambidextrous. In his little league days, he switch-pitched! He threw three innings left-handed and three innings right-handed. In American Legion ball, he played second base as a righty, but third base as a lefty.

Donnie Baseball

In 1987 Mattingly achieved his most incredible feat. He hit three grand slam homers in less than two months. He also hit 11 home runs in an eight-game run, with at least one in each game. That eight-game homer streak broke the AL record and left him tied with the all-time record.

In the final years of his career, Mattingly hit .288 three times and .304 once. He'd suffered some injuries that cut into his playing time in 1990 and 1993. His battles with the Yankee owner George Steinbrenner were famous, and the Yankees never even won their division during all 15 years of his playing time. "It's tough when you have a club that can win, and you're losing," he once said. After the 1995 season, Mattingly decided to retire because of back problems.

CAREER STATISTICS

Batting average	.307
At bats	7,003
Hits	2,153
Doubles	442
Triples	20
Home runs	222
Runs scored	1,007
Runs batted in	1,099
Walks	588

Willie Mays

Willie Howard "Say Hey" Mays is third on the all-time home run list behind only Hank Aaron and Babe Ruth. He hit 660 in his career, hitting over 40 in six seasons and over 50 in two. He posted a career batting average of .302 and is one of only three players to compile 500 home runs and 3,000 hits. He was inducted into the Hall of Fame in 1979.

Willie Mays was born in Westfield, Alabama, on May 6, 1931. He was the oldest of 12 children. His athleticism was natural. His mother had been a sprinter, and his father played baseball, starring for the local league.

A Rocky Start

Willie played for a local team and then signed on with the Giants. In 1951 he was batting .477 for their Triple-A team, so they brought him up to the big leagues. He had a tough time adjusting to major league pitching. He went 0-for-12, hit a home run that flew faster and farther than anyone had ever seen, then went 0-for-13. He broke into tears in the dugout and asked to be sent down, but manager Leo Durocher wouldn't hear of it. He loved Willie's fielding and was sure that his hitting would come around. He told Willie that he was going to be the center fielder for the Giants and that was all there was to it.

It was the kick in the pants that Willie needed. He started to hit, actually getting two in the next game, and despite his terrible start, he ended the season with a .274 average and 20 home runs. His energy and enthusiasm were catching, and he quickly became a fan and team favorite. Spirits were high on the Giants because of Willie Mays, and it was a large part of the reason they won the pennant that year. The Yankees had a rookie of their own in the lineup during that World Series with the Giants. His name was Mickey Mantle.

> Say Hey Willie earned his nickname because "say hey" was his hello to everyone he saw. A large part of this was his inability to remember people's names.

Ball Player Sent to Battle

But it all quickly came to an abrupt halt. Willie Mays had barely begun when the Korean War came knocking. He played only 34 games in 1952 and missed all of 1953 while fighting for his country. It's almost certain that he would have moved ahead of Babe Ruth on the home run list if he'd had those two additional years.

In 1954 he came back full force and took the batting crown and the MVP award. His batting average that year was .345, and he slugged 41 home runs. He won the MVP award again in 1965, batting .317 with 52 homers. He was one of the top six vote getters for the MVP award for 12 years!

The Giants moved to San Francisco in 1958, and Willie won those fans over, too. Many people have described Willie Mays as a real-life representative of the perfect baseball image. Even as a professional, he was the perfect eager "little leaguer," always smiling, always rushing out onto the field because he couldn't wait to play. Players and fans alike couldn't help but catch his love for the game.

Fan Favorite

The country was also eager to accept Mays because he was a black player who wasn't angry and defiant the way Jackie Robinson was. A personality like Jackie Robinson was vital for baseball's racial pioneer, because the baseball world had to respect him. It was a must. But Robinson was hard to embrace. Willie Mays, on the other hand, was completely open and lovable. He was the first black player to become a hero to all races.

Toward the end of his career, he turned into a mentor and a peace-maker for the blacks who followed him into the game. Once, the manager of the Giants made some incredibly racist remarks: "We have trouble winning because we have so many Negro and Spanish-speaking ballplayers on this team." The team was outraged. A group, including the club's owner, wanted the manager fired. Mays organized a private meeting. He pointed out that the firing would only turn the manager into a hero for rednecks. It was better just to let him go at the end of the season. Things were smoothed over.

On top of his spectacular performances at the plate, Willie Mays added phenomenal fielding and a sense of showmanship to his game. With a combination like this he couldn't help but become a New York hero. He used to wear a cap that was two sizes too big. He felt it added a lot more drama to his catches when it flew off his head. He hardly needed it. He once caught a 475-foot fly ball to center *with his bare hand*!

In the first game of the World Series, Willie made a tremendous catch to keep the Cleveland Indians from winning. A ball was hit deep to right-center, almost surely going to drop for a triple. Mays turned and sprinted, his back to the ball. He held his glove out without breaking stride and snagged it out of the air. To top it off, he whirled around and fired the ball to the second baseman, which forced the runner tagging from second to hold up at third.

One of the Best Ever

In 1970 Mays crossed the 3,000-hit border, becoming the tenth player ever to do so. Oddly enough, he just barely missed being the ninth, as Hank Aaron beat him to it. Willie Mays is ninth overall, however, on the total hit list with 3,283.

Though his offensive production began to slide toward the end of his career, Mays still had the respect of opposing pitchers. With over 600 lifetime homers, they knew he could turn a game around with one swing of the bat. Their caution was displayed in 1971, when at age 40 Mays led the NL in walks with 112. He hit 18 home runs that season, and also stole 23 bases in 26 attempts.

A Curtain Call in New York

Willie returned to New York for his final two seasons. He was traded to the Mets and was able to play in front of the same fans he did

when he began his career. Though he played sparingly, his veteran experience and advice to younger players helped lead the Mets to the World Series. He retired after the postseason.

Willie Mays was one of the most exciting offensive players in the history of baseball. His aggressive swing at the plate combined with his great running speed allowed him to hit for average and power. Mays treated every at bat as if it might be his last, and he had fun on the field. His enthusiasm and amazing talents made him one of the most popular players to ever play the game.

CAREER STATISTICS

Batting average	.302
At bats	10,881
Hits	3,283
Doubles	523
Triples	140
Home runs	660
Runs scored	2,062
Runs batted in	1,903
Walks	1,463

Willie McCovey

Willie Lee "Stretch" McCovey is tenth on the all-time home-run list, with 521 under his belt. He led the league three times in home runs, three times in slugging average, and two times in RBIs. He was inducted into the Hall of Fame in 1986.

Willie McCovey must have intimidated nearly every pitcher he came across. He was 6'4" and 220 pounds of pure muscle. He could crush any pitch, and did so with regularity.

Too Much Talent

Nevertheless, McCovey had a rocky start in the majors. He did well in the minors, but there was no place for him on his major league team, the San Francisco Giants. They already had a young slugger named Orlando Cepeda, who played first base. Willie's numbers in the minors were just too good to ignore, so he was brought up, anyway, to platoon at first with Cepeda. Both of them also played outfield with rather poor results.

But McCovey had a real problem with the platoon because he was losing the battle for first. He had good numbers, but Cepeda's were better. But fate stepped in. Cepeda injured his knee and was promptly traded to St. Louis. It was time for the "other Willie" on the Giants to make his mark.

Grand Slams Galore

In the peak of his career, 1963 to 1970, Willie hit over 30 home runs in seven out of the eight seasons. Three of those years he was leading the league. He also hit 18 career grand slams, which puts him second only to Lou Gehrig. In the 1971 pennant battle, he was one of the series heroes, batting .429 and clubbing two home runs. Despite his efforts, however, the Giants lost to the Pittsburgh Pirates.

He did get one memorable chance at the world championship with the Giants in 1962, but unfortunately it wasn't the kind of memory he wanted. The scenario was one that every little leaguer imagines in his or her mind. It was the seventh game of the World Series, bottom of the ninth, two outs. The team was losing by one run, but there was a man on second. McCovey was up at bat. He connected solidly for a line drive toward right field. "The hardest ball I ever hit," said McCovey. The second baseman reached up, made a grab for the ball, and the series was over. The Giants had lost, and McCovey had lost his moment of glory.

Going into his final season, Willie McCovey needed just one home run to tie the great Ted Williams on the career homer list. Though he played very little, McCovey smacked his 521st to ink his name alongside "The Splendid Splinter."

McCovey led the NL in slugging percentage from 1968 to 1970. He had his best season at the plate in 1969 and won the NL MVP award. He batted .320, with 45 home runs and 126 RBIs.

In 1974 McCovey was traded to the San Diego Padres, and his Hall of Fame numbers began to drop. He returned to the Giants in 1977 and won the NL Comeback Player of the Year, hitting .280, with 28 dingers. He retired in 1980.

CAREER STATISTICS

Batting average	.270
At bats	8,197
Hits	2,211
Doubles	353
Triples	46
Home runs	521
Runs scored	1,229
Runs batted in	1,555
Walks	1,345

Fred McGriff

Frederick Stanley McGriff is the Atlanta Braves first baseman. He's had seven seasons with more than 30 home runs, hitting over 20 for every full season that he's played. He's hit over 90 RBIs for six straight seasons.

Little Freddie

Fred McGriff was a little surprise trick-and-treat package for his parents on Halloween in 1963. He had two brothers and two sisters, but the closest one to him was seven when he was born. So little Freddie McGriff had to play a lot by himself. He'd play base-ball. If there was no one to play with, he'd set the ball up on the tee and swing all day long by himself.

In every breath, he inhaled baseball. He spent every moment he could watching the Big Red Machine during their spring training in Tampa. If he wasn't watching them, he was playing baseball himself, pickup games, little league games, and imaginary games in his head. His friend once said, "The only time he'd play other sports with us was just to get in shape for baseball."

An Early Showdown

With a baseball obsession like this, it would make sense for Fred to have been a superstar at a young age, but he wasn't. He didn't make the high school team until he was a junior. He was little and skinny and wore glasses. Nobody expected much from him. Then, in his senior year, he grew. He was 6'3" and weighed almost 200 pounds. People started to pay attention. Fred really caught their eye, though, when he played a rival team from the other side of Tampa. The pitcher was Dwight Gooden, and he already had a famous fastball. The two locked up in a pitcher-to-hitter battle that many locals still talk about today.

Gooden threw him a pitch and McGriff, according to some sources, blasted it 500 feet. Scouts were there looking at Gooden, and all of a sudden, McGriff was a hot prospect. The Yankees picked him in the ninth round of the draft. Fred's parents thought their son should go to college, but Fred's mind was made up, so off he went to play rookie league ball.

Top-prospect Yankee first basemen, including Don Mattingly in Double-A ball, were lined up in front of McGriff, and he was beginning to think he'd made a mistake. Toronto thought otherwise, sensing something the Yankees didn't. They traded for McGriff cheaply, and his career was off and running. Yankee owner George Steinbrenner has since said, "We've made some deals over the years that didn't turn out, but I'm not sure if there was a worse one than that."

Sometimes in the middle of the night, Fred's wife will wake up and see him out of bed swinging the bat. According to Fred's mother, he's been doing it ever since little league. He watches his swing in the mirror, analyzing every little portion. "Sometimes, when I'm struggling, I've just got to do it," he says. "I want to find out what I'm doing wrong, and then I can go back to sleep."

Crime Dog Delivers

In 1988, McGriff's first full season as the Toronto first baseman, he hit .282 with 34 home runs. He scored 100 runs and brought in 82. The following year he led the league in homers, with 36, and knocked in 92 more runs. As a free agent McGriff signed first with San Diego, becoming the highest-paid player in Padre history, and then with Atlanta. In San Diego he proved his contract was worth it. His homers were over 30 and his RBIs over 100 every year. In Atlanta the numbers were close to the same. In the 1995 World Series McGriff was a leader on and off the field for the Braves. He slugged two home runs and led the team to a world championship.

CAREER STATISTICS

Batting average	.285
At bats	5,693
Hits	1,622
Doubles	291
Triples	19
Home runs	339
Runs scored	946
Runs batted in	1,007
Walks	880

Mark McGwire

Mark David McGwire is the 6'5" prolific right-handed slugger for the St. Louis Cardinals. In 1997, he hit 58 home runs, putting him tied for fourth on the all-time single-season list. With his 52-homer total in 1996, he became only the second player in baseball history to have back-to-back 50 home run seasons.

Mark McGwire has hit double-digit home runs for nearly every full season he's played. His total was 387 at the end of the 1997 season, and if he remains injury-free, he's capable of breaking any home run record. He lost almost all of 1993 and 1994 to the disabled list and parts of 1988, 1989, 1992, 1995, and 1996 as well. He was ten home runs away from breaking Roger Maris's record in 1996, and when he hit 58 in 1997 had to adjust to NL pitching. If he stays put and injury free, Maris's record might be in danger.

Bayside Basher

Mark McGwire was born on October 1, 1963, in Pomona, California. He went to college at USC and did what he does best. He set the conference record for most homers in a season with 32. In 1984 the Oakland Athletics grabbed him in the first round of the draft. In his first full season with the A's, he announced his arrival in the majors with a bang. In fact, 49 bangs. He led the league in home runs, home run percentage, and slugging average. His 49 homers were a rookie record, and he was chosen as Rookie of the Year by a unanimous vote. It was the second time in history that that has happened. (Carlton Fisk was the first.)

The next year was strong but not quite as spectacular. Mark hit 32 home runs and 99 RBIs and missed the end of the season because of back stiffness. He returned in time for the World Series, and while the A's lost their bid for the championship, Mark had one of the highlights of his career. In the ninth inning of game three, he homered to give the A's the 2-1 win.

In 1989 he hit 33 home runs, and in 1990 he hit 39. He became the first player in history to hit more than 30 home runs in each of his first four years. In 1992 he led the league in slugging average and home run average and hit 42 home runs, one short of the lead.

Even though Mark was in the running for the single-season home run record in 1996, he chose to miss a game when his son was born.

Scary When Healthy

Then Mark's injuries took over. He was out with heel and back problems for much of 1993 and 1994. When he came back in 1995, though, all his rehabilitation had made him stronger. The season was shortened by 44 games because of the contract negotiations, and Mark missed 33 other games because of injuries, but he still managed to slug 39 homers. He did this in a mere 317 at bats, which put him at the top of the all-time list for single-season home run percentage. The next year saw him topping the all-time list for fewest at bats to hit 40 home runs and fewest to 50. The baseball world is waiting to see what Mark will do with a full season.

What makes McGwire so fun to watch is not just that he hits home runs, it's how high and how far he hits them. A large number of his home runs travel over 400 feet, and sometimes even 500. He hit one off Seattle's Randy Johnson that traveled 539 feet! Fans who sit in the upper deck often get a souvenir when Mark McGwire is at the plate.

CAREER STATISTICS	
Batting average	.260
At bats	4,622
Hits	1,201
Doubles	198
Triples	5
Home runs	387
Runs scored	811
Runs batted in	983
Walks	890

Joe Medwick

Joseph Michael "Ducky" Medwick hit over .300 for 14 of his 17 years in baseball. In 1937 he topped the charts in every hitting category but triples: batting average, slugging percentage, at bats, hits, doubles, home runs, runs, and RBIs.

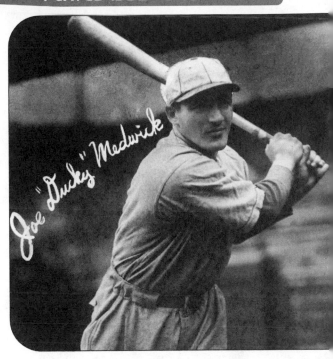

Joe Medwick began his career with the St. Louis Cardinals. The Cardinals in those days were referred to as the Gashouse Gang. Their personalities caught the attention of the fans. They were sloppy, young jokers, but fast, daring, and eager to win. And they did win, taking the pennant in 1930 and 1931 and the World Series in 1934. Joe Medwick did his part, batting .379 in that series.

Bad-ball Hitter

But the 1934 series wasn't his only claim to fame. In Joe Medwick's first ten seasons he batted over .300, getting over 200 hits four of those years. He had the reputation for going after bad balls, usually something pitchers like to hear. Joe, however, took those bad balls and turned them into hits. In 1940 he was traded to Brooklyn. He was hit in the head by a pitch, which some say had a permanent effect on his game. He still managed to hit over .300 six out of the next nine years, and he retired with an average of .326. He was inducted into the Hall of Fame in 1968.

CAREER STATISTICS	
Batting average	.324
At bats	7,635
Hits	2,471
Doubles	540
Triples	113
Home runs	205
Runs scored	1,198
Runs batted in	1,383
Walks	437

Johnny Mize

*J*ohn Robert "the Big Cat" Mize is eighth on the all-time list for slugging percentage. He led the league in home runs four times and RBIs three. Despite being a slugger, he could also hit for average. He retired with a .312 batting average. He was inducted into the Hall of Fame in 1981.

A Slow Rise to Stardom

When Johnny Mize was signed to play for a minor league team, scouts said he would never make it to the majors. Boy did he prove them wrong.

Mize batted over .300 in his first nine seasons. In those seasons and one more after that, he also knocked in over 100 RBIs. He came close to earning the Triple Crown twice. His real claim to fame is being the only player to sock three home runs in a game six times!

Mize missed the '43, '44, and '45 seasons due to World War II. He came back with a vengeance. He topped the charts in home runs in 1947 and 1948. In 1949 he was sent to the Yankees and spent the last five years of his career winning the World Series with them. He was the series MVP in 1952.

CAREER STATISTICS

Batting average	.312
At bats	6,443
Hits	2,011
Doubles	367
Triples	83
Home runs	359
Runs scored	1,118
Runs batted in	1,337
Walks	856

Paul Molitor

Paul Leo Molitor is the Minnesota Twins designated hitter. He tripled on September 16, 1996, to become the 21st player to reach 3,000 hits, the first ever to do it with a triple. He's eleventh on the all-time hit list and still going. He's also fourteenth on the all-time doubles list.

Paul Molitor started his life in Minnesota and decided to end his career there, signing with the Twins in 1996. He thought he would notch hit number 3,000 after a couple of years and then retire. He was 40 years old and had played in the big leagues for 18 years. The year before had been the worst of his career. His .270 batting average was well below his normal .300. In his mind, he was nearing the end.

Saving His Best

But the hometown fans must have sparked something inside him, because 1996 was Paul Molitor's best year ever. He banged out 225 hits to lead the league, and had a batting average of .341. It was the highest hit total he'd ever had. He reached his 3,000 mark on September 16, well before his first season with Minnesota was over. He became only the second player since 1950 to knock in over 100 RBIs while having fewer than ten home runs. Far from the decline he anticipated, Molitor was on top of the world.

His start in the majors was something of a surprise, too. When Robin Yount was having a mid-career crisis, trying to figure out if he wanted to play baseball or professional golf, Molitor was called up from the Milwaukee Brewers minors to replace Yount at shortstop. Then the Brewers owner Bud Selig had a chat with Yount and was sure he'd resign. Molitor was sent back to the minors without playing a single major league game.

A Big Leaguer for Good

All of a sudden, Yount disappeared from spring training and the Brewers yanked Molitor back. This time he made it to the majors. On Opening Day, he started at shortstop. He got a single in his first game, and he homered in the next. Finally, in May, Yount returned to the club, but Molitor had already impressed everyone. Yount went back to shortstop, but the Brewers kept Molitor on, repositioning him at second. They were glad they did. Molitor hit .273, with six homers and 30 stolen bases, the club high. He was voted the AL Rookie of the Year.

After being pushed over to second base by the returning Robin Yount, Paul Molitor got used to being shuffled. He has since played every defensive position except for catcher in his long career.

His hitting has gotten stronger ever since. He's had 11 seasons where he's hit over .300, six of them over .320. He's broken the 200-hit mark four times, leading the league in 1991, 1993, and 1996. He's led the league once each in doubles and triples. In 1987, he hit safely in 39 games, the longest since Pete Rose hit in 44 straight in 1978.

Better with Age

In 1993 Molitor had another incredible year. At 37 he finally totaled over 100 RBIs, making him the oldest player ever to have a first 100-RBI season. He led the league in hits, with 211, and he had a .332 batting average. He also hit over 20 home runs for the first time and became the oldest player ever to have 20 home runs and 20 stolen bases in one season. And, finally, after playing for 15 years, Molitor hit a home run against the Brewers, giving him at least one home run against every team in the AL. That same season Molitor won his first world championship as the Blue Jays defeated the Philadelphia Phillies in six games. To no one's surprise, Molitor was awarded the series MVP.

CAREER STATISTICS

Batting average	.307
At bats	10,333
Hits	3,178
Doubles	576
Triples	109
Home runs	230
Runs scored	1,707
Runs batted in	1,238
Walks	1,049

Joe Morgan

*J*oe Leonard Morgan is one of the best second basemen to ever play the game, and he holds several records for that position. He was the NL MVP in 1975 and 1976. He was inducted into the Hall of Fame in 1990.

Even though Joe Morgan was born in Texas, he became a California boy at a young age. He was not a big man, standing only 5'7", but he knew how to generate a lot of power from his compact frame. He used his size to every advantage. He was selective at the plate, and pitchers had a hard time hitting his smaller strike zone. He led the league in walks four years and is third on the all-time list for walks. He's also eighth on the all-time stolen-base list.

The Chicken Flap

Joe began his career with the Houston Astros. He had trouble remembering to keep his elbow high when he was at bat, so his hitting coach taught him to flap his left arm while he was waiting. It was all he needed. His first year he came in second in the Rookie of the Year voting, but he had 14 home runs and 100 RBIs to his credit. He also led the league in walks.

Despite his strong start, Joe had a tough time getting his career off the ground. His knees kept getting in the way. In 1966 he fractured his kneecap, which forced him to miss about a third of the season. Two years later he was out for all but ten games when he tore ligaments in his knee.

The Total Package

Finally, in 1969, he was back in full form. He returned with a vengeance, hitting, walking, stealing bases, and scoring runs. He scored over 100 runs in seven of the next eight years, leading the league in walks twice. During that time he usually stole between 50 and 70 bases a year.

Little Joe Fuels the Big Red

During the peak of his career, Joe was traded to "the Big Red Machine," also known as the Cincinnati Reds. In the mind of the country, this team was the perfect example of baseball at its best. They won their division by 20 games in 1975 and looked clean-cut and All-American. In the 1970s, that alone was quite an achievement.

Joe Morgan was the engine that drove "the Big Red Machine." The two years that this Cincinnati team became the World Champions, 1975 and 1976, Morgan was the NL MVP. In 1975 he hit .327, with 17 home runs and 132 walks. That year he also had the hit that drove in the winning run in the ninth inning of game seven of the World Series. In 1976 he hit .320, with 27 home runs and 114 walks. He was the only second baseman in the history of baseball to win the MVP award two years in a row.

Morgan finished his 22-year major league career in Oakland following the 1989 season. He hit his 268th career homer there, which then was the most hit by any second baseman in baseball history. Morgan was elected to the Hall of Fame in 1990.

In 1983 Joe Morgan was reunited with former Cincinnati Reds teammates Tony Perez and Pete Rose. The trio led the Philadelphia Phillies to the World Series, where they lost in five games to the Baltimore Orioles. The Phils were nicknamed "the Wheeze Kids," playing off the 1950 Phils, who were called "the Whiz Kids." Morgan, Perez, and Rose were at the end of their careers, and the nickname poked fun at their ages.

CAREER STATISTICS

Batting average	.271
At bats	9,277
Hits	2,517
Doubles	449
Triples	96
Home runs	268
Runs scored	1,650
Runs batted in	1,133
Walks	1,865

Eddie Murray

Eddie Clarence Murray is a switch-hitting first baseman and designated hitter. He's a slugger near the top of many all-time lists. He's fifteenth on lifetime home runs, seventh on lifetime RBIs, eighth on lifetime total bases, and tenth on the all-time hit list. He's second only to Lou Gehrig for career grand slams.

Eddie Murray was born on February 24, 1956, in Los Angeles, California. Five Murray boys (Eddie was the fourth) played in professional baseball at some level. Eddie and his brother Rich were the two to make it to the majors. Together they have the third-highest brother homer total in history. Rich contributed four to that total.

A Star-studded Squad

Eddie starred in both baseball and basketball during high school, but baseball success was in the family, so that was the way he went. On his high school baseball team were three other major leaguers: brother Rich, Ozzie Smith, and Gary Alexander. Eddie was signed by the Baltimore Orioles in 1973.

He made it to the major leagues in 1977, wowing the Orioles and the rest of the league with his 27 homers, 88 RBIs, and .283 batting average. He was voted Rookie of the Year. The next two years, he put up numbers similar to his rookie year, and in 1980 he broke the .300 mark in batting average, the 100 mark in RBIs, and the 30 mark in home runs.

The following year, 1981, was a strike-shortened year, but Eddie still managed to slug 22 home runs. His RBI total of 78 led the league, and he tied for the league lead in home runs.

A Banner in Baltimore

Eddie led the Orioles to a world championship in 1983, batting .306, hitting 33 home runs, and driving in 111 RBIs. Those were team highs in every category. He played five more years with the Orioles, hitting close to or over .300 and having home run totals in the double digits. Nobody ever said he wasn't consistent.

Eddie Murray played in 160 or more games five times in his career, playing every single inning of every single game in 1984.

When he was traded to the Dodgers in 1989, nothing changed. He led their team in nearly every hitting category with his same consistent numbers, hitting his career-high batting average of .330 in 1990.

On April 21, 1994, Eddie Murray set an incredible record. He hit homers from both sides of the plate in the same game for the eleventh time in his career. It was the most in baseball history. Mickey Mantle had held the previous record of ten.

Three's Company

He notched hit number 3,000 on June 30, 1995 in Minnesota, and on September 6, 1996 he joined a club whose only other members were Willie Mays and Hank Aaron. He became the third player in history to have 3,000 hits and 500 home runs. The year 1996 also marked the twentieth consecutive season where Murray brought in 75 or more RBIs. That broke Hank Aaron's record of 19, putting Murray at the top.

Eddie was voted an All-Star eight times and finished in the top ten in league MVP voting eight times. In 1982 and 1983 he came in second in the MVP vote. His consistency and endurance have made him one of the game's best players.

CAREER STATISTICS

Batting average	.287
At bats	11,336
Hits	3,255
Doubles	560
Triples	35
Home runs	504
Runs scored	1,627
Runs batted in	1,917
Walks	1,333

Stan Musial

Stanley Frank "Stan the Man" Musial is one of the top hitters the game of baseball has ever seen. He's fourth on the all-time total-hits list, third on the doubles list, sixth on the runs list, and fifth on the RBI list. He had 18 seasons batting over .300, and he retired with a career batting average of .331. He was inducted into the Hall of Fame in 1969.

"Stan the Man" Musial began his baseball career in 1940 as a pitcher in the St. Louis Cardinal minor leagues. He was pitching and batting well and hopeful that it would turn into something more. On one of his off days, he was playing the outfield and dove for a catch, injuring his pitching arm. That marked the end of his pitching career.

A High-flying Card

The end of his pitching career did not mean it was the end of his baseball career. The Cardinals had also watched Stan Musial hit. They put him in the outfield, and the rest is history. For the next 17 years, he hit over .300 (his first season he hit .426, but he only played in 12 games). At the end of 22 years Musial was still a Cardinal, and he had notched 3,630 hits, hit 475 home runs, won the batting title seven times, and had six 200-hit seasons.

Stan Musial lost only one year to World War II. He wasn't drafted because he had so many kids. Finally, in 1945, he did serve one year with the navy. He took a year off in 1945 to go to war, but other than lowering his career-hit total by about 200 hits, it didn't affect him at all. He came back in 1946 and won the batting title with a .365 average and also led the league in hits, on-base average, doubles, triples, and runs.

In 1948 Musial missed the Triple Crown by one home run. He officially had 39 that year, but he actually had hit the one more he needed in a game that got rained out. It was also that year that he went 5-for-5 against the Dodgers in one game, and 11-for-15 in that whole series. Of those 11, four were doubles, one was a triple, and one was a home run. In 1954 he turned in an even more impressive show. In a double-header against the Giants, Musial hit five home runs!

A Few Lucky Fans

On May 13, 1958 Stan Musial had 2,999 hits. Breaking that 3,000 mark has always been a big deal, but it was even more of a big deal back then when only seven other players had done it. Stan and the team decided that they wanted the moment to happen in front of the hometown fans, so he decided to sit out that May 13 game against Chicago. The news was out, so only about 6,000 fans showed up for the game that afternoon at Wrigley Field. But as the game was winding down, the Cardinals were behind 3-1. The coach needed Musial in there. He pinch-hit for the pitcher, and there it was: number 3,000! The 6,000 scattered fans and very few press people were the only witnesses to this great moment.

Stan Musial ended his career well after that moment, with 3,630 total hits. Unbelievably, his hits were divided exactly equally between his home and away games. He had 1,815 hits at home and 1,815 away.

In a tight game against the Cubs in Musial's first year in the majors, he found himself on second base when an ump made a bad call against the Cubs. They started arguing, but they hadn't called time out. Musial used the moment to race to third and then home. When they finally noticed what he was doing, it was too late. He had already scored the winning run. That's heads-up baserunning.

CAREER STATISTICS

Batting average	.331
At bats	10,972
Hits	3,630
Doubles	725
Triples	177
Home runs	475
Runs scored	1,949
Runs batted in	1,951
Walks	1,599

Tony Oliva

PLAYED 1962–1976

Pedro Oliva y Lopez was the Minnesota Twins outfielder for 15 years. He led the league in hits five times, collecting over 200 of them twice. He led the league in doubles four times, and won the batting crown three times. He was the first rookie to ever win the league batting title. He retired with a lifetime average of .304.

Anytime, Anyplace

Tony Oliva was born in Cuba on July 20, 1940. He started playing baseball as a young boy, grabbing games whenever and wherever he could. It didn't matter if he was playing with kids or adults, as long as they would have him. And if he didn't have a team, he'd create one, grabbing four of five kids and going to an empty lot. He didn't even need a ball. "In Cuba, if we didn't have a ball to play with, we'd scrounge around and perhaps come up with a bottle cap. It was round and we could throw it and hit it. If you can hit something as small as a bottle cap, think what you could do to a baseball."

Tony left Cuba just in time, before Fidel Castro closed the door, and signed with the Twins. They played him in the majors a total of 16 times in 1962 and 1963, but he showed them he was big league material when he batted over .400 both of those years. In 1964 he was brought up for good, and he was ready. Oliva arguably had the greatest rookie season in baseball history. He became the first rookie to win the major league batting title. He hit .323 and collected 217 hits, also tops in the league. That year he also led the league in doubles, with 43 and runs, with 109. On top of that, he launched 32 home runs and knocked in 94 runs. Needless to say, he was voted Rookie of the Year.

The Pride of Cuba

The next year was just as impressive. Tony won the batting crown again and also continued to lead the league in hits, which he did five times in seven years. In 1969 he hit .385 in the league champion-ship series in the Twins efforts to win the pennant. In 1970 he went 6-for-12 in the playoffs, hitting .500. The following year he topped the league in batting average for one last time.

By now his knees were bothering him. In 1972 he could only play in ten games. Fortunately, the AL decided to add the designated hitter. Tony Oliva hit the DH's first home run in 1973. He played that position for the next three years, and led the league in pinch-hitting average with .538.

His aching knees also drained Oliva of some of his power. Without being able to use his legs at full strength, he couldn't generate the power to hit the long ball with consistency. He retired in 1976, staying with the Twins as their hitting coach. He was instrumental in helping out the development of young hitters in the Twins organization. One of them was former all-star Kirby Puckett. His philosophy is part of baseball legend. "It don't mean a thing if you ain't got that swing."

Tony's only World Series appearance came in 1965 when the Twins faced the Los Angeles Dodgers. Minnesota fell victim to one of the greatest pitching performances in World Series history. After losing game two, Sandy Koufax threw a complete game shutout in game five. He came back three days later in game seven to shut out the Twins again. Koufax went all nine innings, and allowed just seven hits over his final 18 innings.

CAREER STATISTICS

Batting average	.304
At bats	6,301
Hits	1,917
Doubles	329
Triples	48
Home runs	220
Runs scored	870
Runs batted in	947
Walks	448

Mel Ott

Mel Ott was a New York Giant outfielder for 22 years. He banged out 511 homers, leading the league for six of his playing years. He led the NL six times in walks and finished his career with a lifetime average of .304.

A Giant Step

Mel started playing professional ball at a very young age. He was signed by the Giants in 1926, when he was only 17. His first couple of years were spent mostly on the bench, but when he started playing full-time in 1928, he proved he belonged in the lineup every day, launching 18 homers that year.

In the 1933 World Series Ott became a hero. In the first inning of the first game, he blasted a two-run homer into his favorite place, the right field stands of the Polo Grounds. Then in the tenth inning of the final game, with the score tied 3-3, Ott smacked another one out of the park. The Giants won the World Series.

Ballpark advantage or not, Ott became the first player in the NL to hit over 500 home runs, leading the league in home runs six times in his career. In 1929, his highest home run year, he hit 42 dingers, but that year he didn't top the list—Chuck Klein beat him with 43. Ott was notorious for his high leg kick as he strided into the pitch. Though players are often seen doing it today, Ott was one of the first to use it.

CAREER STATISTICS

Batting average	.304
At bats	9,456
Hits	2,876
Doubles	488
Triples	72
Home runs	511
Runs scored	1,859
Runs batted in	1,861
Walks	1,708

Rafael Palmeiro

Rafael Corrales Palmeiro is the Baltimore Orioles first baseman. In three out of the last four years, he driven in more than 100 RBIs and belted over 37 home runs. Palmeiro is a career .294 hitter.

Rafael Palmeiro was born on September 24, 1964, in Havana, Cuba. His family moved to Miami when Rafael was 7, but his brother, José, had to stay behind. He was close to military age, and the Cuban government wouldn't let him go. For 21 years Rafael didn't see his brother, but in 1992 they finally were able to get together.

A Star Is Born

Rafael grew up near Miami Stadium, where the Orioles had their spring training. He used to watch them play and chase down home run balls hit by his superstar idols. In high school Rafael was a baseball star himself, earning MVP honors his senior year. He then went on to Mississippi State, where he was All-American and won the first Triple Crown in the conference. He was drafted by the Cubs in the first round in 1985.

He played two partial seasons of outfield with the Cubs and in the minors and then was brought up full-time in 1988. That year Palmeiro finished second in batting average, hitting .307, and second in doubles, with 41. In 1989 the Cubs traded him to Texas, where he became their full-time first baseman.

An Offensive Machine

In his five years with Texas, he led the league in hits in 1990 with 191 and had over 200 hits in 1991. Those two years his average was .319 and .322, respectively. He had double-digit home runs every year but one, and more than 20 each year for the first three. He led the league in doubles and runs scored once each, and in 1990 he was named the Ranger's Player of the Year.

Despite his success, Palmeiro couldn't reach a contract agreement with Texas. He was a free agent, so they decided just to sign Will Clark to play first base and let Palmeiro fend for himself. Rafael was furious. He was in the middle of building a house near the Texas stadium. He'd planned on building a life there, too. But there was nothing he could do.

Rafael Palmeiro wasn't the only major league prospect on his Mississippi State squad. Will Clark and Bobby Thigpen were teammates with Palmeiro and also went on to have successful careers in the major leagues.

Fortunately, the team he'd loved as a child wanted him badly, and he signed on as their first baseman, becoming the eighth Cuban player on the Baltimore team. His three-year batting average with the Orioles has been over .300. In his first year he got on base safely, through a hit or a walk, in 32 consecutive games. For a chunk of the season he had been on base 101 out of 111 games. In 1995 he slugged a career-high 39 homers. A year later, he did it again and broke an Orioles record by driving in 142 runs. He won the Most Valuable Oriole award two years in a row. And that's on a team with names like Ripken, Alomar, Anderson and Mussina.

Palmeiro had a slow start in 1997. He was mired in a slump for the first couple months of the season, but as great hitters always do, he found his stroke. He finished with 38 homers and 110 RBIs, leading the Orioles to the AL Eastern Division title.

CAREER STATISTICS

Batting average	.294
At bats	6,097
Hits	1,792
Doubles	360
Triples	31
Home runs	261
Runs scored	963
Runs batted in	958
Walks	656

Tony Perez

*A*ntanasio "Tony" Perez
played for 23 years in
the major leagues. He won
five division titles in seven
years with the Cincinnati
Reds. He totaled 2,732
career hits and 379 home
runs and drove in 1,652
runs. He played in the
World Series five times and
retired in 1986.

Tony Perez was born on
May 14, 1942 in Camaguey,
Cuba. He began his major
league career with the Cincinnati Reds in 1964 at 22.
Though he saw some time at
first, it wasn't until 1967 that
Tony started playing full-time.
He batted .290 while clouting 29
home runs and driving in 102 runs. He
was in the lineup to stay.

Tony was known as a clutch-hitter, and
his 1,652 career RBIs are proof of his
ability to hit with runners on base.
Driving in runs became second nature
to Perez. His years hitting in the middle
of the lineup for "the Big Red Machine"
gave him plenty of RBI opportunities.

Perez and the Reds went to four World
Series in seven years from 1970 to 1976,
winning the world championship in
1975 and 1976. Perez hit three home
runs in the 1975 series, including a two-
run shot in game seven. Tony also
played for Montreal and Boston before
appearing in the 1983 World Series with
the Phillies. He returned to the Reds in
1984 and retired in 1986.

CAREER STATISTICS

Batting average	.279
At bats	9,778
Hits	2,732
Doubles	505
Triples	79
Home runs	379
Runs scored	1,272
Runs batted in	1,652
Walks	925

Mike Piazza

Michael Joseph Piazza is the catcher for the Los Angeles Dodgers. His lifetime batting average is .339. He has hit over 20 home runs and over 90 RBIs in each year of his short career. If anyone is going to be the next triple crown winner, it could very well be Mike Piazza.

Mike Piazza was born on September 4, 1968, in Norristown, Pennsylvania, one of five brothers. Growing up, Mike was obsessed with becoming a ball player. His heroes were the Phillies third baseman Mike Schmidt and the immortal Babe Ruth. He used to hit baseballs against a mattress propped up against a wall in his basement.

Put Him in a Cage

His dad realized Mike's potential and built him a makeshift batting cage in the backyard. He bought a pitching machine for the nine-year-old, and from that point on Mike Piazza took 300 swings a day out there, even in winter. "I wasn't blessed with a lot of talent," says Mike. "Nothing came easy for me. I had to work to perfect my skills."

When Mike was 13, Tommy Lasorda, a Piazza family friend and coach of the Los Angeles Dodgers, let him be the batboy for the team when they were in Philadelphia. He also pitched to him and saw what he could do. He started making plans to have Mike on his team. In the 1988 draft, Lasorda finally was able to persuade the Dodgers to draft him, but only after promising them that Piazza would be a catcher, not the first baseman that he was in high school. They picked Piazza in the 62nd round, the 1,389th choice.

The Best 62nd-Round Pick Ever

It took four years in the minors for Piazza to learn to catch, but it was worth it. In 1993 he arrived in Los Angeles for his rookie year. He batted .318, with 35 homers and 112 RBIs. It was more than enough for him to win the Rookie of the Year award, the fourteenth Dodger to do so. He's equaled or bettered those stats every year since then. In strike-shortened 1994 he hit .319, with 24 homers. In 1995 he hit .346, with 32 homers. In 1996 he hit .336, with 36 homers and 105 RBIs.

Piazza has used his off-season time to "go Hollywood." He's been on Baywatch, The Bold and the Beautiful, and Married . . . with Children. He was turned down for a part in the Robert DeNiro movie called The Fan. It was for the part of a major league catcher. They didn't think he was convincing enough!

A Homecoming Blast at the Vet

Being selected to play in an All-Star Game is an outstanding achievement. But when Mike was selected to be the NL's starting catcher for the 1996 All-Star Game, it had even greater meaning. The game was played at Veterans Stadium in his home state of Pennsylvania. Piazza didn't disappoint his friends and family at the game when he blasted a home run into the upper deck in left-center field.

Unfortunately, his new position as catcher isn't the easiest on his body. The Dodgers gave him a break in 1996 and played him occasionally in other positions, but Piazza likes being behind the plate. He has been compared to the great catchers of the past, yet he's modest about his achievements. *Beckett Baseball Card Monthly* wanted him to pose with pictures of Johnny Bench and Roy Campanella. Piazza wouldn't do it. "I don't see myself in that class at all. They did it their whole career . . . I have much more to accomplish."

CAREER STATISTICS

Batting average	.339
At bats	2,558
Hits	854
Doubles	110
Triples	3
Home runs	168
Runs scored	423
Runs batted in	538
Walks	272

Kirby Puckett

Kirby Puckett was the Minnesota Twins center fielder and the heart of their team until 1996. He had five seasons where he totaled 200 or more hits. In eight of his 12 years, he hit over .300. He was forced into early retirement in 1995 because of glaucoma. He retired with a lifetime batting average of .318.

Kirby Puckett was born in the projects of Chicago on March 14, 1961. He was the youngest of nine children. His father worked two jobs, and his mother watched over the children, making sure none of them got into drugs or gangs. Kirby's love was baseball right from the start. He played whenever he could, making balls out of socks, aluminum foil, or whatever he could find.

Keeping the Dream

Kirby's father died in 1981, and Kirby was going to quit school to help the family out. His mother refused, saying she'd invested too much in his baseball to let him stop. It turned out to be a good investment. Kirby's mother died in 1989, but she saw her son play in the majors and saw him take the Twins to the World Series.

Puckett began his pro career in 1982, playing in the minor leagues of the Twins organization. Word soon spread that a super center fielder was hitting .382 in his first year. In 1984 the Twins decided to bring him up. His teammates had heard about his hitting accomplishments, but they were unprepared for what they saw. Kirby was not the typical long, lean center fielder. He was 5'6" and about 200 pounds. But he was fast, and he could hit. Puckett figured his body helped him to get where he was. "You have to have quick wrists to drive the ball, but I think I get a lot of my power from my thighs and my butt."

He proved that in his first game in the majors. His first time up, he grounded out, but he got a hit in each of the next four at bats. He went on to hit .296 that year and won the Rookie of the Year award.

The Power of Puckett

In 1986 he really hit his stride. He hit .328, with 223 hits. The next year he hit .332 and led the league with 207 hits. The Twins advanced to the World Series and won the world championship in an exciting seven games. Kirby hit .357 in his first World Series. He didn't stop there, leading the league in hits again for two more years in a row and winning the batting crown in 1989. In nine of his 12 years, he also hit home runs in the double digits.

Kirby's nicknames are many. He's been called Puck, Stub, Fire Hydrant, Fire Plug, Buddha, Pit Bull, Cannonball, Cannonball Head, Hockey Puck, Bucket Head, and Minnesota Squats.

Puckett led the Twins back to the World Series in 1991. They were matched up against a tough Atlanta Braves team and were trailing the series three games to two. Game six went into extra innings, but a home run by Puckett sent the series to game seven. Minnesota won that one, too, and captured another championship.

In spring training of 1996, tragedy struck. Kirby realized that he was having difficulty seeing. He could see around the edges of things but not what was directly in front of his eyes. He had glaucoma. After five unsuccessful surgeries to try to correct the problem, Kirby retired from baseball, nearly blind in one eye. He isn't bitter about it. "I don't have any tears about this. Every day I wake up, and I thank God I woke up. I thank God we caught the disease in my left eye . . . I knew that one day it was inevitable, that the baseball would be over . . . There's a time for everything."

CAREER STATISTICS

Batting average	.318
At bats	7,244
Hits	2,304
Doubles	414
Triples	57
Home runs	207
Runs scored	1,071
Runs batted in	1,085
Walks	450

Jim Rice

*J*ames Edward Rice was a
Boston Red Sox slugger who
also hit for average. He retired
with a .298 lifetime batting
average, having topped the charts
three times in home runs.

When Jim Rice began playing full
time in the big leagues in 1975, he
handled the pressure well. He hit
.309, with 22 home runs and 102
RBIs. He won the Rookie of the
Year award and helped Boston
advance to the World Series.

Replacing Legends

But when the Red Sox decided to
move him to left field, it created even
more pressure. He would be replacing the
legendary Carl Yastrzemski, who replaced the
legendary Ted Williams. Could Rice fill those
cleats? Only time would tell.

As before, when Yastrzemski replaced
Williams, the Red Sox obviously knew what
they were doing. In his first year as the Red
Sox starting left fielder, Jim Rice hit .320, with
39 dingers. His slugging average and home
run total topped the league. He had 206 hits
and drove in 114 RBIs. The following year he
did even better. He led the league in slugging
average, home runs, hits, triples, and RBIs.
His batting average of .315 was great, too, but
not quite great enough to get him the Triple
Crown. Rod Carew hit .333 that season.

Rice had another great season in 1983,
leading the league in homers with 39. But he
was having problems with his eyesight. He
eventually had to retire in 1989.

CAREER STATISTICS	
Batting average	.298
At bats	8,225
Hits	2,452
Doubles	373
Triples	79
Home runs	382
Runs scored	1,249
Runs batted in	1,451
Walks	670

Cal Ripken Jr.

Calvin Edwin Ripken Jr. is the shortstop and third baseman for the Baltimore Orioles. He holds the all-time record for consecutive games played. His lifetime average is .277, and he's hit 370 home runs in his career.

Baseball's Savior

Known as the man who saved baseball from itself, Cal Ripken Jr. is a modern-day hero to most baseball fans. After baseball had a disastrous off-season with players and owners battling over contracts, the start of the 1995 baseball season was in jeopardy. Replacement players could be found at spring training. It was questionable whether the players would ever find themselves back on the field. The fans were furious.

Cal Ripken had his own set of worries, on top of his career security. He was chasing Lou Gehrig's consecutive game streak of 2,130 games. If a replacement player took his spot at shortstop at the start of the season, then his streak would be over, just short of Gehrig's. Fortunately, the owner of the Baltimore Orioles refused to hire replacement players. Baltimore would not put a team on the field until the dispute was settled.

As it turns out, there wasn't a single replacement player who ever saw playing time, anyway. The owners and players came to an agreement, the season's Opening Day was pushed back, and Cal Ripken showed up at his regular spot at shortstop.

Enter, the Man of Steel

Still, the fans were disgusted at both the owners and the players. The feeling was that they were all a bunch of whining millionaires who were ruining the game and charging high prices at the same time. Ballparks remained half full for most of the season, and no one was very interested in baseball news. Then along came Cal. As Lou Gehrig's record came closer, fans started watching. Ripken was a hard-working family man who seemed to live for baseball rather than the money he could make from it. The fans embraced him as a sign that old-time baseball values still had a chance.

Cal's first major league stolen base was a steal of home. It was a double steal, where his teammate was stealing second at the same time.

On September 6, 1995, Cal Ripken took the field for his 2,131st consecutive game, breaking Lou Gehrig's record. The crowd gave him a standing ovation that seemed to go on forever. Just to make a great night a perfect one, Ripken homered in his record-breaking game.

A Perennial All Star

Cal began this tremendous streak on May 30, 1982, his first full year in the majors. By the end of the season, he had hit .264, with 28 home runs and 93 RBIs to win the Rookie of the Year award. He had only missed three games all season. Not a bad start.

He has never missed another game since. In 1983 he hit .318 and led the leagues in hits with 211, doubles with 47, and runs with 121. He was voted the AL MVP, and the Orioles went on to win the World Series that year.

The remainder of Ripken's years have been solid and consistent. His knowledge and experience at the plate make him a threat at any time. In 1991 he won his second MVP award, hitting .323, with 34 home runs and 114 RBIs. At the end of the 1997 season he had 2,715 career hits and 370 home runs. He is quickly closing in on hit number 3,000 and home run number 400.

CAREER STATISTICS

Batting average	.276
At bats	9,832
Hits	2,715
Doubles	517
Triples	43
Home runs	370
Runs scored	1,445
Runs batted in	1,453
Walks	1,016

Frank Robinson

Frank Robinson is fourth on the all-time home-run list, with 586. In 17 of his 21 years, he hit over 20 of them, leading the league in 1966 with 49. That year he won the Triple Crown and the MVP award. He was the first player to win an MVP award in each league. He was inducted into the Hall of Fame in 1982.

A Young Gun

Frank Robinson began his major league career with the Cincinnati Reds in 1956. It was a good start. He led the league with 122 runs, and slugged 38 homers while batting .290. He earned the Rookie of Year award and was on his way to a great career. He continued to belt over 30 homers for ten of his seasons, and he averaged over .300 nine times.

In 1961 Robinson and the Reds won the pennant. That year Frank led the league in slugging average, and hit .323, with 37 home runs and 117 RBIs. He won his first MVP award. Except for a dip in his numbers in 1963, Robinson continued to put in an all-star performance. Nonetheless, the Reds general manager decided he had peaked. He figured he'd better trade Robinson while he could still get something good back. Robinson went to the Baltimore Orioles.

Never Doubt Mr. Robinson

The Reds general manager was wrong. Frank Robinson got to the Orioles and promptly won the Triple Crown. Doing that, he also won another MVP award, making him the first player to win the award in both the National and the American Leagues. He led the Orioles to the World Series and hit two home runs, helping them win the Fall Classic.

With Baltimore, Robinson went to three more World Series. He also had three more seasons over .300 and five more double-digit home run years. More importantly, Robinson displayed outstanding leadership skills. This is something that would assist him when his playing career was over. In the last years of his career, he bounced around, playing for the Dodgers, the Angels, and the Indians, turning in solid performances wherever he went. He hit 30 home runs with the Dodgers in 1972, and drove in 97 runs with California in 1973.

In his rookie year, Frank Robinson had the distinction of being the player who was hit by the most pitches.

Chief of the Dugout

Finally, in 1975, he took the helm of the Cleveland team and became baseball's first black manager, 28 years after Jackie Robinson (no relation) broke baseball's color barrier. He was one of the last few player/managers. In his first game as a player/manager, Robinson smacked a home run. He obviously made the right decision by putting himself in the lineup.

In 1976 Robinson was closing in on career-hit number 3,000. He would have joined Aaron and Mays as the only players to compile 3,000 hits and 500 home runs. But after a lengthy career, Robinson felt his skills were diminishing. He took himself off the roster to keep from hurting the team. He retired with 2,943 hits, just 57 short of 3,000.

CAREER STATISTICS

Batting average	.294
At bats	10,006
Hits	2,943
Doubles	528
Triples	72
Home runs	586
Runs scored	1,829
Runs batted in	1,812
Walks	1,420

Jackie Robinson

Jack Roosevelt Robinson is famous for having broken baseball's color barrier. On top of that, he was also an excellent hitter. He was Rookie of the Year in 1947 and MVP in 1949. He retired with a .311 batting average and was inducted into the Hall of Fame in 1962.

When Jackie Robinson was born on January 31, 1919, his parents probably had no idea what a tremendous difference their youngest son was going to make in the game of baseball and in the country.

Four-Sport Star

In high school, Jackie was already becoming a superstar athlete. He played baseball, football, and basketball, and ran track. Then he went on to UCLA and participated in the same four sports, becoming the school's first four-letter athlete. So Jackie had a taste of what being first was like.

Jackie Robinson began playing major league baseball in 1947 with the Brooklyn Dodgers. At the time, there wasn't a single black player in the game, and there hadn't been for more than 50 years.

Robinson was not exactly welcomed by everyone. The St. Louis Cardinals threatened to strike if he played (he did and they backed down). Many of the whites in the crowds booed him. Players on other teams insulted him. Everyone called him names. But the president of the Dodgers, Branch Rickey, had chosen Jackie to be the first black ballplayer because he knew Jackie could handle the pressure.

Robinson not only handled the pressure, he thrived on it. In his first year he hit .297 and notched 175 hits. He also led the league in steals. That year baseball decided to add a Rookie of the Year award, and Jackie Robinson was its first winner. In 1987 the award was actually renamed the Jackie Robinson award, but the name has never really stuck and people still call the winner "the Rookie of the Year."

Two years later, in 1949, Jackie Robinson was also voted the league's MVP. He took the batting crown with a .342 average and knocked in 124 RBIs with 203 hits. And again, he led the league in steals.

Blue-chipper

Jackie was a clutch hitter. He obviously was used to acting cool under pressure, so this worked for him in his hitting, too. His hits were primarily line drives, which he could stretch into extra base hits because of his incredible speed.

To show how unhappy they were at a black entering their sport, pitchers on the other team threw right at Jackie when he was up at bat. Even though he dodged most of the pitches, he was hit nine times his first year.

He helped the other hitters, too, by making the pitchers nervous every time he was on base. They never knew if he was going to steal or not. More likely than not, he would. He even stole home 19 times in his career. Sometimes he would fake a break to the next base just as a pitch was delivered. This would pull all the infielders out of position, and Jackie's teammate at the plate could easily find the hole in the infield.

Giant Killer

The 1951 pennant race proved just how valuable Jackie was to the team. The Dodgers had blown a 13-game lead over the New York Giants. They were down to the last day of the season, and if the Dodgers lost again, the pennant would go to the Giants. The game was tied in the ninth inning. A ball was hit toward Robinson. He dove for it and made an incredible rolling catch to keep the game tied. Then in the 13th inning Robinson blasted a homer to win the game for the Dodgers.

Jackie Robinson died in 1972 of diabetes. He was only 53 years old, and partially blind, but he'd lived long enough to see the game fully integrated.

CAREER STATISTICS	
Batting average	.311
At bats	4,877
Hits	1,518
Doubles	273
Triples	54
Home runs	137
Runs scored	947
Runs batted in	734
Walks	740

Alex Rodriguez

Alex Rodriguez is the Seattle Mariners shortstop. He is the third player in the history of baseball to begin a season at age 20 and end the season as batting champion. The others were Ty Cobb and Al Kaline. Rodriguez accomplished it with an average of .358.

Baseball 101

Alex Rodriguez was born in New York City on July 21, 1975, and was drafted at age 17 to play for the Seattle Mariners. He decided a baseball career made more sense than college because he only got a combined score of 910 on his SATs. The reading comprehension part was tough for him, since his family only spoke Spanish in his home growing up.

The Mariners started playing him full-time at the end of 1995 when Alex was only 19. His average was a not-very-impressive .232, but he was showing potential. He'd hit five home runs, two triples, and three doubles. His strikeout totals were high, but he was lacking major league experience.

Crowned at Age 20

Rodriguez didn't learn to reduce his strikeouts, but he did improve rather dramatically. They started him in the number-nine slot in the lineup (pretty standard for shortstops in the AL), but he was hitting .300. The manager, Lou Piniella, moved him up to the third spot, in front of Ken Griffey Jr. For the rest of the season, Rodriguez hit .370. He ended it hitting .358, winning the batting crown. He also drove in 123 runs and hit 36 homers. That's better than any 20-year-old has done in the history of the game. Even his teammate Ken Griffey Jr. didn't do as well. At 20, he hit .300, with 22 home runs and 80 RBIs.

Even though 1996 was Rodriguez's first full year, he couldn't win the Rookie of the Year award because he played in too many games in 1995. "I don't care about that since I got to be on our play-off team last year, and I wouldn't have traded that experience for ten rookie awards."

Alex Rodriguez, who was given the nickname A-Rod by his teammates, was the first shortstop to win a batting title since Cleveland's Lou Brodeau won it in 1944.

As good a hitter as he is, Rodriguez feels that his fielding is more important to the team. He'd "rather go hitless and make some good plays to help the team win than go 4-for-4 and lose. Nothing justifies an error."

Even though his fielding is very important to the Mariners' success, his production with the bat is hard to overlook. Besides winning the batting title in his first full season in the big leagues, he also led the AL in runs scored (141), doubles (54), and total bases (379). Rodriguez finished second in hits (215), fourth In slugging percentage (.631), and eighth in RBIs (123). Alex has already proved his worth as the number one pick overall in the 1993 draft.

He backed up his title winning season with a solid performance in 1997. He hit .300 on the nose and smacked 23 homers. Rodriguez was selected to the AL All-Star team, an honor he will undoubtedly enjoy many times in the future.

CAREER STATISTICS

Batting average	.332
At bats	1,330
Hits	441
Doubles	100
Triples	6
Home runs	64
Runs scored	266
Runs batted in	226
Walks	106

Pete Rose

Peter Edward "Charlie Hustle" Rose is the all-time hit leader, with 4,256. He is second for doubles, fourth for runs, and tenth for walks. He has played in more games and had more at bats than any other player in the history of baseball. He is banned from baseball for gambling and is currently ineligible for the Hall of Fame.

Baseball's Hit King

Pete Rose is not just a member of the 3,000-hit club. He is president of his class. With his 4,256 hits, he blows the competition away. He has 65 more hits than Ty Cobb was able to notch, and no one else is even at the 4,000-level. He had ten 200-hit seasons, also the highest in the game. Cobb had nine. Like Cobb, a large part of Pete Rose's success was his ferocious drive. As one coach said, "If he got two hits, he wanted three. Get three hits, he wanted four. He kept coming at them, coming at them, never stopped."

He led the league in hits seven times. He also led in batting average three times, with 15 seasons over .300. His lifetime batting average was .303, which would have been a lot higher if he hadn't stayed in the game so long. Of course, his big fame comes from having been in the game so long, so it's a good thing he did.

Dangerously Dedicated

Young Pete Rose had his love of baseball implanted into him by his accountant father Harry Rose. Harry loved baseball, so Pete did, too, and he worked hard to become good at it. That was about all he worked at, though. He flunked ninth grade. He was given the choice of repeating the year or going to summer school. Summer school meant missing a season of baseball. He repeated the year. The attention to baseball paid off, however. He was signed by the Cincinnati Reds in 1960.

He moved to the majors in 1963, getting two hits in his first game. Despite winning the Rookie of the Year award, there was no indication that he would turn into one of the game's greatest hitters. But Pete Rose put his all into baseball, working hard to improve his stroke every day. He loved the game. As he said, "I'd walk through hell in a gasoline suit to keep playing baseball." His diligence earned the nickname "Charlie Hustle" and a Hall of Fame batting style. By his third season, Rose had found his swing, broke .300, and was on the road to superstardom. His philosophy, "see the ball, hit the ball" seems much too simple for a man who worked so hard. Rose won world championships with the Reds in 1975 and 1976, and also with the Phillies in 1980. He won the NL MVP award in 1973.

When Pete Rose was a boy, his father had him swing a bat 200 times every night before bed. Because he was a switch-hitter, he took 100 swings righty and 100 swings lefty.

A Man Possessed

Despite one tremendous season after another, Rose never felt he could let up. He thought that his skill and success were due entirely to hard work rather than his own natural ability. And maybe they were. In his own words, "Baseball is a hard game. Love it hard, and it will love you back hard. Try to play it easy and ease off, and the the first thing you know, there you are, on the outside looking in, wondering what went wrong."

In the end it did go wrong for Pete Rose, but it happened after he retired. He was found guilty of gambling. After the 1919 Black Sox scandal, there was no doubt as to what would have to happen to Rose. The commissioner banned him from baseball for life. As long as he is banned from the sport, the doors at the Hall of Fame will remain closed to Pete Rose.

CAREER STATISTICS

Batting average	.303
At bats	14,053
Hits	4,256
Doubles	746
Triples	135
Home runs	160
Runs scored	2,165
Runs batted in	1,314
Walks	1,566

Babe Ruth

George Herman "Babe" Ruth, also known as "the Bambino" or "the Sultan of Swat," could arguably be the best player ever to play the game. He is second on the all-time home-run list. He is tenth on the all-time average list. He is first in walks. He is second in runs and RBIs. He was one of the five original inductees into the Hall of Fame in 1936.

Babe Ruth's life and career sound like something that Hollywood may have created. Abandoned by his parents as a youth, he grew to be a much-loved baseball hero who changed the face of the game. Small stories about him grew into legends, and his feats on the diamond spoke for themselves. He was truly an American hero.

Tailor-made Hitter

Ruth's early years were tough. His father owned a Baltimore saloon, and young George lived above it until he was seven. It was not the best place for an impressionable young boy, and he easily picked up bad habits, like stealing and chewing tobacco. His parents decided to place him in a school for difficult boys called St. Mary's Industrial School. He trained to be a tailor and was in and out of the school several times during the next 12 years, although he stayed there almost permanently when his mother died when he was 13.

To keep Ruth out of trouble, one of the teachers at the school got him playing baseball. The teacher told him to play as much as he wanted, as long as it didn't interfere with the classroom. Ruth played all the time. He joined several teams and played every position. His teacher soon saw that he had real talent and got Babe a tryout with the Baltimore Orioles. They liked him, signed him, but then soon sold him to the Boston Red Sox in 1914.

When he started playing professional baseball, he was a chubby-faced 19-year-old. His looks and enthusiasm for baseball and the big city had his teammates calling him "Baby." Later it was just shortened to "Babe."

A famous story has Ruth autographing a ball for a seriously sick child named Johnny Sylvester. He wrote, "I'll knock a homer for you on Wednesday." In typical Babe Ruth style, he hit three. Johnny Sylvester lived to see his eighties.

King of the Hill

Incredibly, his first years with the Red Sox were as a pitcher. And he was a tremendously talented pitcher to boot. He had two 20-win seasons and pitched 29 scoreless innings for the Red Sox in the 1916 and 1918 World Series, helping them become World Champions both of those years. When he came up to bat, he was also turning in tremendous performances as a hitter. But as a pitcher, Ruth was only playing every fourth day. The manager was beginning to think he might be more valuable to the team playing every day. He cut his pitching in half, and Ruth responded by leading the league in home runs two years in a row.

The Yankees wanted Babe Ruth, and they had good timing. The Red Sox owner needed money. He sold Babe Ruth to the Yankees for a record amount, over $100,000. At the time, it was a huge amount, more than twice that which any other player had previously gotten. The sale was to haunt the Red Sox forever. The Babe went on to create a Yankee dynasty, winning seven pennants and four World Championships, making them the most successful team in history. The Red Sox have never won a World Series since. Fenway fans refer to it as "The Curse of the Bambino."

The Babe Invents the Long Ball

Even if the trade was bad for the Red Sox, it was good for the Yankees, and great for baseball. The sport had just been dealt a blow by the 1919 Black Sox scandal and no longer held the special glow as "the national pastime." Fans were losing interest. But this slugger called Babe Ruth was drawing attention. He was hitting the long ball, something that previously hadn't been part of baseball. In 1919 he hit 29 of them. The year before, he'd led the league with only 11, so 29 was obviously an incredible number for those days. People decided that this new guy might be worth another look. In every city he played, the fans would come in record numbers.

Babe didn't disappoint. The next year he hit 54 home runs! That was more than any other *team* could put together. The year after he slugged 59! Baseball was reborn, and it had a whole new look. Other players were trying the power game, too. Suddenly, the home run was the high point of baseball. Fans turned out in the thousands to see their favorite players slug one over the wall. And Babe Ruth was a big fan favorite. He led the league in home runs 12 out of the next 14 years. The only reason he wasn't on top the other two years, 1922 and 1925, was because he was only playing half a season.

> *In the third game of the World Series in 1932, Babe Ruth created one of baseball's most enduring moments. Taunted by the Chicago fans, Babe pointed to the bleachers. He made it clear that he intended to send a home run their way. Five pitches later he launched one right where he said he would.*

Bringing Down the House

The Yankees had been using the Polo Grounds, the ballpark of the New York Giants, to play their home games. But with the crowd that Ruth was bringing in, the Yankees took a risk and built the 70,000-seat Yankee Stadium. On Opening Day, appropriately against the Boston Red Sox, it was sold-out. As he stepped up to the plate for the first time, Ruth knew what to do. He took a swing and walloped the ball over the wall. The stadium was quickly nicknamed "The House that Ruth Built," and the right-field bleachers were soon called "Ruthville." The left-handed Sultan of Swat continued to deposit balls there with regularity.

But in 1925, Ruth got a scare. He had been a big partier, drinking and staying up all night, even right before games. It never seemed to affect him, until right before the 1925 season. He collapsed at a train station and spent many weeks in the hospital with intestinal problems. He didn't get back to baseball until June. His numbers in that partial season weren't up to his usual standards, but the season was an important one to him. He went back to training regularly and took the game seriously.

The work paid off. Two years later, in 1927, he broke his own single-season record by hitting 60 dingers. The Yankees knew what a gem they had, and they paid him well. He was baseball's first highly paid star. His salary in 1930 and 1931 was even higher than the president of the United States was getting. Ruth could justify it, though. "I had a better year than he did."

He had five more years with his homer totals in the forties and fifties, and then he started to decline. In 1934 the Yankees let him go. Ruth was able to sign on for one season with the bottom-scraping Boston Braves, but his playing days were over.

Ruth knew how to go out in style, however. After a pathetic start to the season, he once again made history at Forbes Field in Pittsburgh. In that game he blasted home runs number 712, 713, and 714. The last one sailed out of the park, something that had never before happened at Forbes Field. Ruth retired a week later.

CAREER STATISTICS

Batting average	.342
At bats	8,399
Hits	2,873
Doubles	506
Triples	136
Home runs	714
Runs scored	2,174
Runs batted in	2,211
Walks	2,056

Tim Salmon

Timothy James Salmon is the right fielder for the Anaheim Angels. He is the only player in the club's history to have four seasons with 30 or more home runs.

Raised in Arizona

Although Tim Salmon was born in Long Beach, California, and now plays for the Anaheim Angels, he thinks of Arizona as his home. He played baseball in high school in Phoenix, Arizona, hitting .381 with a .905 slugging average. His feats attracted the attention of the majors. He was selected in the 1986 draft by the Toronto Blue Jays, but he went to college instead and signed with the Angels in 1989.

He made his major league debut in 1992, and although he homered three days later, he struggled at the plate. He had a sore wrist, though, and the manager insisted he get a cast on it. That ended his season.

But 1993 came along and Tim turned in a Rookie of the Year performance. He hit .283, with 31 home runs and 95 RBIs. He set a club record by hitting 23 of those homers in Anaheim. He hit .500 in the last 18 at bats of the season and ended that year with his first grand slam.

On Fire

His second year with the team was the year of the baseball strike. While his numbers were lower because of it, he had an incredible streak in May. In three straight games he went 4-for-5, 4-for-5, and 5-for 5. Only three other AL players have ever gotten 13 hits in only three games. Salmon hit seven singles, two doubles, one triple, and three home runs.

He had another stellar year in 1995. He hit .330, breaking .300 for the first time, slugged 34 home runs, and drove in 105 runs. He did all this in only 143 games and became the first Angel to hit over .300, hit 30 homers, and knock in over 100 RBIs in the same season.

Salmon experienced similar success in 1997. He batted .296, crushed 33 homers, and knocked in 129 runs. This was after a slow start. Although his strikeout total was still high (142), he had a career high in bases on balls (95).

At 6'3", 200 pounds, Salmon looks like he'll be a solid offensive player for a long time. In addition to his size and talent, Salmon has Hall of Famer Rod Carew as his hitting instructor. With natural-born skill and the advice of a hitting legend, Salmon is a potential threat to any opposing pitcher.

It's surprising that Tim Salmon isn't more timid at the plate. He's had bad luck with wild pitches in college. One year he was hit by a pitch, and it broke his nose. The following year he got hit by another pitch, and it broke his jaw.

In the majors his body has been pretty abused, too. He was hit when a bat broke and flew into him while he was standing in the on-deck circle. He also broke a bone in his finger when he dove for a ball.

CAREER STATISTICS

Batting average	.293
At bats	2,667
Hits	782
Doubles	143
Triples	11
Home runs	153
Runs scored	464
Runs batted in	503
Walks	426

Mike Schmidt

Michael Jack Schmidt was the Phillies third baseman for 18 years. He is seventh on the all-time list for home runs, with 548. He won eight home run titles, the most ever by a National Leaguer. For 14 seasons in a row, he hit over 20 home runs, and with the exception of 1978, he hit over 30. He was inducted into the Hall of Fame in 1995.

Never Give Up

Mike Schmidt was born on September 27, 1949, in Dayton, Ohio. He was a huge baseball fan, and a good athlete, but his desire was a lot stronger than his ability to play. During his freshman year his hitting was so bad that no summer team would take him. His grandmother, of all people, urged him to keep trying. He did, but he still never won a single baseball award during high school. After he had both his knees operated on, he took off for college, with the advice that he should give up sports. He didn't listen to the doctors, and so his college baseball performance attracted the major leagues. Mike was drafted by the Phillies.

When Mike Schmidt hit the majors, he didn't have a position. The minor league teams had tried him at all four of the infield spots, but he hadn't settled in at any of them. But because of his hitting in the minors, the Phillies knew they wanted him up in the majors. They stuck him at third. He stayed with the Phillies and he stayed at third base for the rest of his incredible career.

In his rookie season in 1973, Schmidt's hitting wasn't that impressive—he was batting .196—but neither were the Phillies. There was not a whole lot of threat to Mike's position on the team. He did manage to hit 18 home runs that year, and his potential impressed the manager. The next year Schmidt proved him right. He hit 36 home runs to lead the league. The next three seasons he hit 38 home runs three times in a row, leading the league twice in 1975 and 1976.

History at Wrigley

It was a game in 1976 that gave him the ticket he needed to join an elite club. On April 17 of that year, he was playing the Cubs at Wrigley Field, and the Phillies were down 12-1 after three innings. In the fifth inning, Mike hit a home run with one man on. Then in the seventh, he hit another one. The score was now 13-7. Fans were beginning to think they might get an exciting game after all. In the eighth inning, Mike belted his third home run, this time with two men on. The score was 13-12. The ninth inning saw the score at 15-15, and the game went into extra innings. In the tenth, Mike Schmidt made history by slugging his fourth home run in one game. The Phillies won 18-16, and Mike joined 11 other players who had hit four in one game.

A Proven Winner

In his career he's won five division championships, two pennants, and one World Series. Before Mike Schmidt, the Phillies won the pennant only twice in their entire history. Both times they were crushed in the World Series. They needed Mike Schmidt. In the 1980 World Series, he batted .381 and hit two homers. They went on to win in six games, and Schmidt was named MVP.

Mike Schmidt is credited with hitting one of the longest singles ever. During a game at the Houston Astrodome, Schmidt hit a towering drive to center field. It looked as if it would be another long home run, but the ball hit a speaker at the back of the dome. It dropped down onto the field, and because of ground rules, the ball was ruled in-play. Schmidt stopped at first with a single.

CAREER STATISTICS

Batting average	.267
At bats	8,352
Hits	2,234
Doubles	408
Triples	59
Home runs	548
Runs scored	1,506
Runs batted in	1,595
Walks	1,507

Mike Schmidt won eight home run titles and four RBI crowns. Three years of his career, he earned the MVP award, and he was also given the Lou Gehrig Award. He set 35 Philadelphia Phillies records, and *Sports Illustrated* voted him the best third baseman of all time.

Gary Sheffield

Gary Antonian Sheffield is the Marlins superstar right fielder. In 1996 he hit well over .300 and slugged 42 home runs. He drove in 120 runs and managed to draw 142 walks.

Baseball in the Blood

Gary Sheffield was born on November 18, 1968, in Tampa, Florida. As a boy, he played baseball every day, going to the neighborhood playground with his uncle, pitcher Dwight Gooden, who was just four years older. Gary played little league in that park, too, leading his team to the Little League World Series. Five of the kids on that team went on to the major leagues.

It wasn't a great neighborhood when Gary was growing up, and it's even worse now, just a decade later. There are drug deals, race riots, and constant police sirens. The little league numbers are way down because many of the kids would rather play the drug game than a baseball game. Gary and his family moved out in 1987, a year after Gary was drafted by the Milwaukee Brewers. When he got his signing bonus, he went a little crazy spending his money. He bought a Mercedes and had his initials in gold embedded into his teeth.

Making a Good Impression

His major league start came in 1988, and it was a doozy. For his first hit, Sheffield crushed a ball off Mark Langston for a ninth-inning homer, which tied the game at 1-1. Then in the eleventh inning, he hit a single to drive in the game-winning run. But after that impressive start, his career didn't do much. From 1988 to 1991, he played in the majors on and off with the Milwaukee Brewers. He never hit over

.300, and only once did he get into the double digits in homers, with ten in 1990. But he did remove the gold GS from his teeth.

In 1992 Sheffield was traded to the San Diego Padres. It was just what he needed. He was their starting third baseman, and he quickly slugged his way to the top. He won the batting crown that year with an average of .330, and he also hit 33 home runs. He knocked in 100 RBIs and scored 87 runs. Then he was traded to the Florida Marlins.

Back to Business

Sheffield had some problems off the field over the next couple of years, but he got It all together in 1996. In the first month of the season, he hit 11 home runs, tying the April record held by Willie Stargell, Mike Schmidt, and Graig Nettles. He was hitting everything.

But pitchers caught on and came up with a new strategy. They wouldn't throw him strikes. So Sheffield starting walking. Before 1996, he'd only walked 55 times at most. By the end of the 1996 season, he had 142 walks. He still managed to tag some bad pitches for hits, though. If it was anywhere near the plate, he was going for it. "I am not trying to walk," he said. "I don't care if I hit .150 with runners in scoring position. I'm going to be aggressive early in the count. It's my only way to drive in runs." It paid off. In addition to his tremendous walk total, Sheffield hit .314, clubbed 42 home runs, and brought in 120 RBIs.

People often ask Gary how he learned to hit so well. He figures it all happened at the playground. "At the park, they'd often make Dwight and me split up, so I got to hit off him. I hit him well, too . . . it goes back to all those games."

Gary Sheffield loves to look good when he's not on the field, and now he has the money to do it. He has over 250 pairs of shoes, and he once turned an entire garage into a closet to hold all his clothes. In the room-size closet in his new home, he's put in a rotating rack like those at the dry cleaners. He does, however, find some more admirable outlets for his money. He gives lots of money to charities, underprivileged kids, and other people in need.

CAREER STATISTICS

Batting average	.286
At bats	3,659
Hits	1,048
Doubles	194
Triples	14
Home runs	181
Runs scored	603
Runs batted in	621
Walks	561

Al Simmons

Al Simmons had six seasons with 200 or more hits, five of them in a row during his peak years of 1929 to 1933. During that time he also led the league twice in batting average and once each in hits, at bats, runs, and RBIs. He retired with a lifetime batting average of .334.

Al Simmons was traded ten times and played with seven different teams during his 21-year career.

Most of his stardom, however, came with the Philadelphia Athletics. It was with them that he had five of his six 200-hit seasons. And he was one of the main reasons they went to three consecutive World Series (1929–1931). In those three seasons, Al batted a phenomenal .365, .381, and .390. His home run totals were 34, 36, and 22.

Bucketfoot Al

His batting style wasn't conventional. He stepped toward third rather than back toward the pitcher. This was called "putting your foot in the bucket" and earned Simmons the nickname "Bucketfoot Al." In his first 11 seasons, he hit over .300 and knocked in over 100 runs every year. Later his numbers would decline a little, but his early excellence allowed him to finish his career with a lifetime batting average of .334.

CAREER STATISTICS

Batting average	.334
At bats	8,761
Hits	2,927
Doubles	539
Triples	149
Home runs	307
Runs scored	1,507
Runs batted in	1,827
Walks	615

George Sisler

Georgeorge Harold "Gorgeous George" Sisler holds the all-time record for number of hits in a single season, with 257. He's fourteenth on the all-time batting average list, retiring with an average of .340. He was elected to the Hall of Fame in 1939.

George Sisler was born on March 24, 1893, outside Akron, Ohio. When he was in high school, he signed to play with the local Akron team for free. After his college career, he played for the St. Louis Browns. He played with St. Louis for all but two of his 15-year career.

Sizzlin' Sisler

In his first full year, he hit .305. That would end up being the second lowest average in all of his 15 years. In 1920 Sisler led the league with a whopping .407 and set the record at 257 for total hits in a season. The record still stands today. In 1922 he hit .420 with 246 hits. That year, he also set an AL record for consecutive games with a hit (41) that lasted until Joe DiMaggio broke it in 1941.

After 1922, Sisler began having trouble with his eyesight because he had infected sinuses. He missed the entire 1923 season. He had one more great year, in 1925, batting .345, but he never returned to his former glory. Sisler hit .309 in his final season in 1930, and hit career home run number 100.

CAREER STATISTICS	
Batting average	.340
At bats	8,267
Hits	2,812
Doubles	425
Triples	165
Home runs	102
Runs scored	1,284
Runs batted in	1,175
Walks	472

Duke Snider

Edwin Donald "Duke" Snider hit over 40 home runs for five straight years. He hit 407 of them in his career and retired with a lifetime batting average of .295. He was the first to hit four homers in a World Series twice. He was inducted into the Hall of Fame in 1980.

Earning His Stripes

Duke Snider started with the Brooklyn Dodgers on the same day as Jackie Robinson, but he didn't have quite as good a first season. The Dodgers sent him down to the minors after 40 games. He had struck out about a third of the time he came up to bat. In the minors, he was forced to watch pitch after pitch without swinging so he could better learn the strike zone.

The New York teams dominated baseball during Snider's time, and the Dodgers and the Yankees were often in the World Series. With Duke Snider slugging away at the plate, the Dodgers went six times. In the 1952 and 1955 series, Snider homered four times. He is fourth on the all-time home run total for World Series games.

Snider retired in 1964. He will forever be remembered as one of four outstanding center fielders to play the game during the 1950s and 1960s along with Mays, Mantle, and Richie Ashburn.

CAREER STATISTICS	
Batting average	.295
At bats	7,161
Hits	2,116
Doubles	358
Triples	85
Home runs	407
Runs scored	1,259
Runs batted in	1,333
Walks	971

Sammy Sosa

PLAYED 1989 – PRESENT

Samuel Sosa y Peralta is the Chicago Cubs right fielder. He's had five seasons of 25 or more home runs. He's had three seasons with over 100 RBIs. In 1993 he joined the elite 30-30 club, with 33 home runs and 36 stolen bases.

A Throw-in Player

Sammy Sosa was born in the Dominican Republic on November 10, 1968. He signed his first pro contract with the Texas Rangers at 16, but it took him until 1989, when he was 21, to get to the majors. Once he was there, Sammy was shuffled from the Rangers to the Chicago White Sox to the Chicago Cubs, with no one giving him a full-time job in the lineup. In fact, Sammy Sosa was just a throw-in in the Wilson Alvarez and Harold Baines deal that the Rangers and the White Sox made. Little did they know how good a player they were allowing to get away.

When Sammy joined the Cubs full time in 1993, he proved his worth. He hit 33 home runs and had 93 RBIs. And the next year, which was a strike-shortened one, was the only year in which he had hit totals that were lower. He's improved every year. If he keeps going up, he'll break every Cubs record in the book.

He's already set a few Cub records. He was the Cubs first-ever 30-30 man, when he hit 33 home runs and stole 36 bases in 1993. He accomplished that same feat again in 1995, when he clubbed 36 homers and stole 34 bases. No one else on the Cubs has ever even come close. They have only had three 20-20 players in their club history.

Free-swinging Sammy

Sammy works hard at batting practice, sometimes doing it three times a day. He uses a heavier bat and a heavier ball when he practices, hoping to increase his strength. And although he's had success, he does have room to improve. He likes the low fastball, but he gets fooled easily on other pitches. And he almost never gets a called third strike on him. In fact, he almost never gets a called first or second strike. Sammy likes to swing the bat.

Sammy Sosa is from a small town in the Dominican Republic called San Pedro de Macoris. This town has produced several other major league players, including Pedro Guererro, Mariano Duncan, George Bell, and Tony Fernandez.

All the kids in Chicago grabbed their gloves and ran out onto Waveland Avenue at Wrigley Field when Sammy came to the plate in 1996. Waveland runs behind the left-field bleachers at Wrigley, and it's where a lot of Sosa's towering fly balls have landed. He clubbed 40 home runs in just 498 at bats and was on pace to hit over 50. But he broke his hand in August and missed the remainder of the season.

A Silver Lining

During 1997 Sosa surpassed the 200-homer mark with his 29th of the season. Sammy blasted 36 dingers and rang up 119 RBIs to cap another great year with the bat. His numbers probably would have been even more impressive, but he was hitting in a weak lineup. If the Cubs can develop a few more dangerous hitters to surround Sosa, pitchers will have no choice but to give him good pitches to hit.

If Sosa has one weakness at the plate, it's chasing bad pitches. He led the NL in strikeouts (174) in 1997 and walked only 45 times. Once he learns to be more selective and lay off pitches out of the strike zone, Sammy's numbers should get even better. The Cubs fans love him now, and they should really love him then.

CAREER STATISTICS

Batting average	.257
At bats	4,021
Hits	1,035
Doubles	162
Triples	33
Home runs	207
Runs scored	593
Runs batted in	642
Walks	277

Tris Speaker

PLAYED 1907–1928

*T*ris "the Gray Eagle" Speaker
stands fifth in two of the
major hitting categories, career
batting average (.345) and total
hits (3,514). He stands alone at
the top of the doubles list,
holding the record with 792. He
won the batting title in 1916,
when he hit .386. He was elected
to the Hall of Fame in 1937.

If Tris Speaker had played baseball
at any other time in history, his
batting record would shine like
silver. However, his major league
career coincided with Ty Cobb's.
Even though Speaker batted over
.360 in eight of his 22 seasons, he
only captured the batting title once.
That was in 1916, when he hit .386
and broke Ty Cobb's streak of nine
straight batting titles. But his record of
792 career doubles has stood since he retired
in 1928.

Show Me the Money

Speaker began his major league career in
1907, playing with the Boston Red Sox. He
took them to two World Series, in 1912 and
1915, but then he moved to the Cleveland
Indians for the 1916 season to get a better
salary. The move was a good one. His first
year there brought him the batting title, and
in 1920 they won the pennant.

He stayed in Cleveland, becoming a
player/manager, until 1926, when he quit
abruptly after being accused of fixing a game
with Ty Cobb. Tris Speaker returned to
baseball for two final seasons, one with the
Washington Senators and one with the
Philadelphia Athletics.

CAREER STATISTICS

Batting average	.345
At bats	10,197
Hits	3,514
Doubles	792
Triples	223
Home runs	117
Runs scored	1,882
Runs batted in	1,559
Walks	1,381

Willie Stargell

Wilver Dornel Stargell played all his 21 years with the Pittsburgh Pirates. He retired with 475 home runs, hitting over 20 in 15 seasons. He was inducted into the Hall of Fame in 1987.

Willie Stargell excelled at both football and baseball. Willie's decision to play baseball was made for him, however, when he broke his pelvis playing football when he was 18. The next year he signed with the Pittsburgh Pirates.

He made it to the majors full-time in 1963. Following his rookie year, he wouldn't hit less than 20 homers for 13 straight seasons. He topped the charts twice in homers, hitting 48 in 1971 and 44 in 1973.

"Pops" Wins MVP

Willie Stargell became the oldest player ever to win an MVP award. He won it in 1979, when he was 39. That year he batted .281, socked 32 homers, and knocked in 82 RBIs. Stargell shined even brighter in the postseason. He hit .455 with two homers in the league Championship Series, and .400 with three home runs in the World Series as the Pirates won it all.

CAREER STATISTICS

Batting average	.282
At bats	7,927
Hits	2,232
Doubles	423
Triples	55
Home runs	475
Runs scored	1,195
Runs batted in	1,540
Walks	937

Bill Terry

Bill Terry was a first baseman for the New York Giants for 14 years. He turned in a career batting average of .341 and had six seasons with over 200 hits and six consecutive seasons where he scored over 100 runs and totaled over 100 RBIs. He was inducted into the Hall of Fame in 1954.

Short but Sweet

Bill Terry's career doesn't have the length of some other Hall of Famers, but it certainly has the numbers. He began his career playing baseball for local teams, but he couldn't get a major league job. Instead he went to work for Standard Oil and played on the company team. It was there that he became a standout and finally got noticed.

He was signed by the New York Giants in 1923, but even then he had to wait until 1927 before he was playing regularly. Then he exploded. He batted over .300 for the rest of his career, and one year, 1930, he even hit .401, capturing the batting title. That year he also set a NL record of 254 hits in a season. With the Giants, either as a player or a manager, Terry won four pennants, and in 1933 the World Series.

Terry also holds a couple of "lasts" in the NL, and that doesn't mean last place. He was the last NL player to hit over .400 in a season and he was the last NL player to retire with a career batting average over .340.

CAREER STATISTICS	
Batting average	.341
At bats	6,428
Hits	2,193
Doubles	373
Triples	112
Home runs	154
Runs scored	1,120
Runs batted in	1,078
Walks	537

Frank Thomas

Frank Edward "the Big Hurt" Thomas is the Chicago White Sox first baseman. He is the only player in major league history to bat .300 or better, with at least 20 home runs, 100 RBIs, 100 walks, and 100 runs scored in seven seasons. Ted Williams and Lou Gehrig accomplished this in four seasons. He won his first batting title in 1997, with a .347 average.

He's called the Big Hurt and is probably the most intimidating hitter in baseball. He can do it all. He leads all active players in career on-base percentage and slugging percentage and is behind only Wade Boggs and Tony Gwynn in batting average.

A Flirtation with Football

Frank Edward Thomas entered the world on May 27, 1968. It was the first time, but hardly the last, that someone thought of him as the Big Hurt. He was first a football star, earning a football scholarship to Auburn University. He played football only his freshman year and then decided to try out for the baseball team. He immediately became a pro prospect and then concentrated on baseball full-time. He holds the Auburn record for most career home runs with 49, and set the single-season record with 21. The Chicago White Sox wasted no time and drafted him in the first round of the 1989 draft.

He only spent a year and a half in the minors, coming to the club in August of 1990. He hit .330 and had seven home runs in the remainder of the season. He never looked back. In 1991 he hit .318 ninth in the league, and with 32 homers, was third. Even though he wasn't tops in those two categories, he still led the league in on-base percentage because of his league-leading 138 walks. He reached base safely in 145 out of 158 games. He came in third in the MVP voting.

Picky at the Plate

His discipline at the plate is incredible. Not only does he collect his league-leading walks, but he can also afford to let marginal pitches go by for strikes while he's waiting for the pitch he wants. He ranks among the top players when batting with two strikes in the count.

During his only playoff appearance, Frank Thomas hit .353 with a home run as the White Sox lost in six games to the Toronto Blue Jays. The amazing statistic, however, is that he drew ten walks in the series.

In 1993 and 1994, he won the MVP award. He is only the eleventh player in AL history to win more than one MVP award in his career. He won it unanimously in 1993, which had only happened nine other times. His 41 home runs in 1993 were a personal and White Sox high, as was his .353 batting average in 1994.

At the end of five years, Frank Thomas had notched 170 home runs. It was the third-highest total at the five-year point in AL history. Joe DiMaggio and Mark McGwire beat him out with 173. To top it off, his sixth year, 1996, was easily the best of his career. He batted .349, with 40 home runs. He scored 110 times and had 134 RBIs. In 1997 his power numbers dropped a bit, but he won his first batting crown. He hit .347 and still launched 35 home runs.

Frank Thomas is what hitting coaches label a "weight shift" hitter. He stays back on the ball and then shifts his weight forward as he swings the bat. This form of hitting enables him to make consistent contact on pitches and keeps his strikeout total down. At the same time, Thomas is so big and strong that he can still hit the ball out of the ballpark. He's truly an all-around great hitter.

CAREER STATISTICS

Batting average	.330
At bats	3,821
Hits	1,261
Doubles	246
Triples	9
Home runs	257
Runs scored	785
Runs batted in	854
Walks	879

Pie Traynor

Pie Traynor, the Pittsburgh Pirates third baseman for all 17 seasons, achieved a career batting average of .320, connected for 2,416 hits, and went to the World Series twice, winning in 1925. Pie was inducted into the Hall of Fame in 1948.

Nothing but a Pirate

All 17 of Pie Traynor's major league years were spent with the Pittsburgh Pirates. After a slow start, his hitting took off after the 1922 season.

In 1923 he totaled 208 hits, an impressive number then and now. He batted .338, and led the league in triples with 19. For ten out of the next 12 years, he batted over .300. In many of those years he knocked in over 100 runs.

Some of his biggest moments, however, came in the 1925 World Series. His average was .346, and he knocked in four crucial runs. In the seventh inning of the seventh game, the Pirates were down by one, with a man on third and two outs. Always a clutch hitter, Traynor crushed the ball into the right-center field gap, scoring the tying run. Traynor tried to stretch an easy triple into a home run to take the lead but was thrown out at the plate. But his play inspired the Pirates on the way to winning the World Championship.

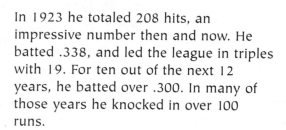

CAREER STATISTICS	
Batting average	.320
At bats	7,559
Hits	2,416
Doubles	371
Triples	164
Home runs	58
Runs scored	1,183
Runs batted in	1,273
Walks	472

Mo Vaughn

Maurice Samuel Vaughn is the Boston Red Sox first baseman. He has hit six grand slams in his short major league career. In each of the past four seasons he's hit over .300 and belted more than 25 home runs. He's made his mark in nearly every Red Sox hitting category.

Seton Hall Legend

Mo Vaughn was born on December 15, 1967, in Norwalk, Connecticut. He went to the exclusive Trinity Pawling Prep School in New York for high school and then went on to Seton Hall University. As a freshman, he broke the school record for home runs. He was All-American all three of his seasons there and was drafted by the Red Sox in the first round of the 1989 draft.

He played large parts of the 1991 and 1992 seasons in the majors, but it wasn't until he was given a full-time job in 1993 that Mo turned it on. He hit .297, with 34 doubles, 39 homers, and 101 RBIs. He hit the first two of six career grand slams. In 1994 he hit .310, with 26 home runs and 82 RBIs.

Then along came 1995. He led the Red Sox in home runs with 39. He tied for first in the AL for RBIs, with 126. He had three grand slams in one season, and he batted .300. Vaughn led the Red Sox to the AL East Division title and an appearance in the postseason. He won the AL MVP, just edging out Cleveland's bad boy, Albert Belle. Now nicknamed "the Hit Dog," Vaughn had officially arrived in Boston.

Not So Nice to Pitchers

Many people, including Albert Belle himself, have criticized the MVP award going to Mo. Mo resents that. "People have said Mo won the MVP because he's a nice guy. Well, I am a nice guy at times, but I play as good as anybody."

Mo Vaughn likes hitting in Fenway Park. He uses the Green Monster as a target when he hits. "I set my sights on the Green Monster in left-center field. I try to hit everything that way. If they throw me inside, I just turn on the pitch."

But there's no denying he's a nice guy. He's set up the Mo Vaughn Youth Center in Dorchester, one of the more disadvantaged areas of Boston. He also does a tremendous amount of community service in the off-season with Boston's youth. And besides, he's just plain friendly to everyone.

If 1995 was good, 1996 was even better. Mo had a .326 batting average, with 207 hits, clouted 44 home runs, and drove in 143 RBIs. He became the first major league player to have 200 hits and 40 home runs in the same season since Jim Rice, another Red Sox player, did it in 1978. Mo also hit the sixth grand slam of his career. Despite a knee injury in 1997, Vaughn had another all-star-type season. He hit .315, with 35 homers.

Just looking at Mo, anyone can see he has the physical tools to be a dangerous hitter. But Mo uses his head as much as his body when he's at the park. Taking advice from guys like Carl Yastrzemski, Jim Rice, and Mike Easler has made Vaughn a versatile hitter. Wherever the pitcher throws the ball, Mo is just waiting to smother it.

CAREER STATISTICS

Batting average	.298
At bats	3,219
Hits	960
Doubles	168
Triples	8
Home runs	190
Runs scored	521
Runs batted in	637
Walks	458

Honus Wagner

*J*ohn Peter "Honus" Wagner hit over .300 in 16 of his first 17 years as a ball player. In the one year he fell short, he hit .299. Eight of those years he captured the batting title. He retired with a lifetime batting average of .327 and collected a total of 3,418 hits. Along with Babe Ruth and Ty Cobb, he was one of the first hitters inducted into the Hall of Fame in 1936.

Coal Chucker

As baseball legend has it, Honus Wagner was signed as a major leaguer when a scout saw him throwing chunks of coal at a train's coal car. The story is essentially true. Ed Barrow was sent by Honus's brother, Albert "Butts" Wagner, to take a look at 19-year-old Honus. Barrow saw all he needed as he watched the coal head toward the hopper like a shot out of a gun. The arm was so impressive that Barrow didn't even give Wagner a batting tryout, feeling that anyone who could throw like that must be a ball player. Barrow's instincts were correct. In Honus Wagner's first season, he batted .338, and he went on to become one of the undisputed greatest shortstops of all time.

Honus Wagner certainly didn't look like the typical lean, fit, athletic ball player. He had a massive barrel chest, probably from working in the coal mines, bowed legs, and arms that were unusually long. But if he didn't have the looks of a typical ball player, he certainly created the look of a superstar.

Though he was known as the best shortstop ever to play the game, Wagner was a great hitter first. He frequently led the league in batting average, hits, doubles, triples, runs, RBIs, and even stolen bases. His hit total, 3,418, set an NL record, which stood for 43 years until Stan Musial broke it in 1963.

World Series Showdown

In classic baseball tradition, there was always the argument over who was the top ball player in the game. During Wagner's era, he was one choice, and Ty Cobb was the other. Everyone compared numbers, but since Honus played in the NL while Ty Cobb played in the AL, it was hard to say if the competition was equal. Wagner supporters hold up their only face-to-face match, the 1909 World Series, as evidence that he was superior. In that show, Wagner outperformed Cobb. He hit .333 and stole six bases. Cobb hit .231 and stole only two bases. It was tempting to say Honus Wagner was the best.

Another way to separate Wagner from Cobb was in his attitude. Wagner was generally liked by teammates and had a humble personality despite his superstar status. He was often helpful in giving advice to teammates. When Honus Wagner retired in 1917, he was 43, his legs were worn out, and his batting average had dipped below .300. But he'd given baseball some incredible years. He left the game having scored more runs, notched more hits, knocked in more RBIs, and stole more bases than any other player had in the history of the NL.

Honus Wagner despised cigarettes, and when he found out that his baseball card was being included in cigarette packs, he made them destroy all the cards they could get their hands on. This makes a Honus Wagner tobacco card the most valuable card in the trading card industry.

Honus was willing to endorse his favorite bats, however. In 1905 he became the first player to put his autograph on a Louisville Slugger bat.

CAREER STATISTICS

Batting average	.327
At bats	10,441
Hits	3,418
Doubles	643
Triples	252
Home runs	101
Runs scored	1,735
Runs batted in	1,732
Walks	963

Lloyd Waner

L loyd "Little Poison" Waner was a rookie phenomenon. He hit well over .330 in his first three years, scoring over 120 runs each season. He led the league in singles four of his first five years and set several rookie-year records, which still stand today.

Lloyd Waner was the younger, smaller version of his older brother Paul. They both played outfield for Pittsburgh and dominated the hit charts during their time. Lloyd played professionally for 18 years, hitting over .300 in 11 seasons. His lifetime batting average is .316.

A Hitter Right from the Start

Despite impressive career numbers, Lloyd is most famous for his phenomenal rookie season. His first year with the Pirates, 1927, he hit .355 and set rookie-year records with 223 hits and 133 runs scored. His 198 singles is a rookie-year record.

The next six years Lloyd also put up big numbers, hitting over .300 every season. And while he wasn't much of a power hitter, he did take advantage of his tremendous speed to turn some doubles into triples. He topped the charts in that category in 1929. He was also tough out at the plate, almost never striking out. In 7,772 career at bats, Waner struck out only 173 times. In 1933 he went down on strikes only eight times in 500 at bats! A truly amazing feat.

CAREER STATISTICS	
Batting average	.316
At bats	7,772
Hits	2,459
Doubles	281
Triples	118
Home runs	28
Runs scored	1,201
Runs batted in	598
Walks	420

Paul Waner

Paul "Big Poison" Waner had 3,152 hits in his 24 years as a major leaguer. He set a NL record by getting 200 or more hits in a season eight different times.

Paul Waner had a great start to a tremendous career with the Pittsburgh Pirates. In 1926, his first year in the majors, he hit .336 and led the league in triples. Some people think his .336 also led the league, but the batting title that year went to Bubbles Hargrave, the catcher for the Cincinnati Reds. Bubbles's average, however, was earned in only 326 at bats. Paul Waner led the league for players who had more than 400 at bats.

Stomping the Sophomore Jinx

His second year was even better. He won the batting title, hitting an incredible .380. That year he also led the league in hits (237), triples (17), and RBIs (131). He never had another year like 1927, but Waner continued to hit over .300 for the next ten years, taking the NL batting title two more times. He ended his career with a lifetime batting average of .333. Not surprisingly, he is one of an elite few players who has amassed over 3,000 hits, totaling 3,152 in his career.

CAREER STATISTICS

Batting average	.333
At bats	9,459
Hits	3,152
Doubles	603
Triples	190
Home runs	112
Runs scored	1,626
Runs batted in	1,309
Walks	1,091

Bernie Williams

Bernabe Figueroa Williams is the center fielder for the New York Yankees. In his short career, he's had four grand slams and has hit a homer from both sides of the plate in four games. He's the only player in major league history to switch-hit homers in a post-season game, and he's done it twice.

Play Me a Song, Dr. Williams

When Bernie was growing up in Puerto Rico, he couldn't decide what he wanted to be. He narrowed the choice down to doctor, guitar player, and baseball player. Those choices are pretty typical ones for kids, but they don't always happen. A child has to work very hard at school, at music, or at sports to make a professional career in one of those fields possible. It's unusual to excel even at one. Bernie excelled at all three.

He was accepted to the Escuela Libre de Musica, which is a high school for budding musicians. Every day after school he worked on his baseball skills with his father. And when he got to college he majored in biology, just in case he took the doctor route.

But then the Yankees approached him about signing. He had to make a decision. He chose baseball. His music teacher was stunned. "I didn't even know he played baseball." His father was thrilled. And Bernie figured, "I can always play guitar or go to college, but I can only play baseball when I'm young." The Yankees couldn't have been happier with his choice.

The Mystique of Center Field

Though his career began at a young age, it took a long time for it to get going. He spent seven years in the minors, being brought up for only short stints in 1991 and 1992. Finally, in 1993, he was brought up for good and placed in the history-packed position of center field. He's been getting better ever since, but it remains to be seen whether he will have the career of DiMaggio or Mantle.

Bernie was discovered by the Yankee scout who was in Puerto Rico looking at Juan Gonzalez. He wanted to sign Bernie right away, but there was a problem. He was only 16 and couldn't be signed until the next year. To keep him out of sight of the other big league scouts, the Yankees gave Bernie an all-expense-paid trip to their summer camp.

If his performance in 1996 is any indication, there's a good chance he will. The Yankees won the World Series, and Bernie was a large part of the reason they did. In the postseason, he hit .345, with six homers and 15 RBIs. In the World Series, they were down 2-0, heading into the third game. By the eighth inning, they were losing that game, too, when Bernie got up to bat. He clubbed a two-run homer, and the Yankees went on to win 5-2. After that, they never lost again, winning the World Series in six games.

During the regular season, he hit .305, with 29 homers and 102 RBIs. He hit two grand slams that year, one of them in a game where he'd previously hit a three-run homer. His eight RBIs that game made him one of only seven Yankees ever to collect eight RBIs in a single game. He batted a career-high .328 in 1997, with 21 homers, 35 doubles, six triples, and 100 RBIs. Bernie can truly do it all at the plate.

CAREER STATISTICS

Batting average	.291
At bats	3,179
Hits	927
Doubles	183
Triples	33
Home runs	100
Runs scored	537
Runs batted in	469
Walks	421

Billy Williams

Billy Leo Williams was an all-around top player. He hit over .300 five times, capturing the batting title in 1972. He led the league in hits and runs in 1970. And in 14 of his 16 full seasons, he hit over 20 home runs. He was inducted into the Hall of Fame in 1987.

Billy Williams didn't star on his high school baseball team like most other hitters who have played the game professionally. He didn't because his high school didn't even have a team. Billy wanted to play, though, so he joined the Mobile Black Bears, which was a minor league team for the Negro leagues. It prepared him well. In 1956, at 18, Williams was signed by the Cubs. They didn't regret it.

In his first full season, Williams hit 25 home runs. He won the Rookie of the Year award and never looked back, hitting over 20 round-trippers for almost every other year he played. He was known to be good in the clutch, and most seasons he hit close to or over .300. His lifetime batting average was .290.

Silent But Deadly

Because Williams played on the same team as Ernie Banks, however, he didn't get as much attention as he deserved. Ernie was the enthusiastic super slugger. Billy was the quietly consistent top hitter. Even though he often outperformed Banks, his modest personality kept him in the background. And because, like Banks, he was playing for the losing Cubs, there wasn't much national attention given to him either.

During his career years of 1970 and 1972, when he led the league in hits or average, he was overshadowed. This time it was Johnny Bench. Both years, Bench was given the MVP award. And both years,

Williams came in second. Banks had even retired by then, so the lack of media attention could hardly be blamed on Mr. Cub's joyful presence.

Mr. Reliable

There was one area, however, where Billy Williams achievements did get recognized. Like Lou Gehrig and Cal Ripken, Billy Williams was a dedicated and reliable player. He set the NL record for most consecutive games, playing in 1,117 of them. This earned him the nickname "Iron Man of the Chicago Cubs."

Billy Williams had such a great swing, it caught the eye of baseball legend Rogers Hornsby. Hornsby, who was a batting instructor in the Cubs farm system, asked that Williams be promoted immediately. Upon his arrival in the big leagues, division rival Willie Stargell describes Williams's swing as "poetry in motion."

At the end of his career, Williams did finally get to play on a winning team. He was traded to Oakland in 1975 and played with them for two years. His 23 dingers for the Athletics helped them to a division title. After the 1976 season, Williams retired, to become a hitting instructor with the Cubs. He was elected to the Hall of Fame in 1987.

Batting average	.290
At bats	9,350
Hits	2,711
Doubles	434
Triples	88
Home runs	426
Runs scored	1,410
Runs batted in	1,475
Walks	1.045

Matt Williams

PLAYED 1987–PRESENT

Matthew Derrick Williams is the Cleveland Indians third baseman. He has 279 career home runs. When he's healthy, he puts up Hall of Fame numbers. He's led the NL in RBIs and home runs and has been elected to four All-Star games, two of which he missed because of injuries.

A Hit from the Start

Matt Williams had his first full season in the majors in 1990, playing for the San Francisco Giants. His numbers were impressive for even a veteran. He led the league in RBIs, with 122. Those RBIs were the most ever by a Giant, breaking Mel Ott's 1938 record of 116. He totaled 171 hits and slugged 33 home runs. He also ripped 27 doubles.

The rest of his career has been similar. In 1991 he hit 34 home runs, with 98 RBIs. The next year was something of a slump, but he still managed to reach the 20-homer mark. The following year he hit a career-high 38 home runs and broke 100 again with 110 RBIs.

Maris Protected by Strike

And then came the strike. Like several other players who have had phenomenal years cut short by strikes, Williams lost out on his bid to break Maris's all-time record of 61 home runs in a season. He hit 43 in the 115-game season, which put him on a pace to equal Maris. He broke the NL record when he hit 33 by the All-Star break. Who knows what might have happened. There's a good chance he would have beaten Hack Wilson's NL record of 56. There's an outside chance he would have topped Maris. But there was also the chance that he'd slump or get injured. Matt was happy with his career-high and league-leading 43 homers.

Nagging Injuries

The following two years injuries really took their toll on Matt, although he hit .336 and had 23 homers in a mere 76 games. He missed quite a bit of the season, including the All-Star game, when he broke a bone in his foot on June 3. He'd swung at a pitch and just barely caught it, sending the foul ball straight down. He stayed up at the plate and singled, but they took him out after he had difficulty running to second. He had pins put in his foot and a cast on it. It was basically the end of his season that year.

In 1996 it was a shoulder injury that shortened his season, but once again he put up good numbers. He hit .302, notched 122 hits, and clubbed 22 home runs. He was traded to Cleveland in the off season, and Matt helped guide the Indians to a division title in 1997. Though he had some trouble adjusting to the pitching early on, he finished strong with 32 homers and 105 RBIs.

A major factor in being a successful power hitter is having good hitters surrounding your spot in the lineup. Matt Williams has been fortunate throughout his career to have some great hitters batting both in front and behind him. Players like Kevin Mitchell, Will Clark, Barry Bonds, David Justice, Manny Ramirez, and Jim Thome are just a few guys who have helped Matt Williams get some good pitches to hit.

CAREER STATISTICS

Batting average	.264
At bats	4,735
Hits	1,249
Doubles	211
Triples	28
Home runs	279
Runs scored	680
Runs batted in	837
Walks	306

Ted Williams

*T*heodore Samuel "the Splendid Splinter" Williams was the last man ever to exceed the .400 batting average mark. Only once in his 19-year career did he hit under .300, and he won six batting titles and two Triple Crowns. He also led the league four times each in home runs and RBIs. He retired with a .344 battling average, putting him sixth on the all-time list. He was inducted into the Hall of Fame in 1966.

Born on August 30, 1918 in San Diego, California, Ted Williams had an unhappy childhood. His mother was a devoted Salvation Army follower, leaving her children home alone, and she often embarrassed Ted by making him march in the band with her. His father was in the army, after which he ran a photo store, then left the family altogether. Fortunately, Ted had an outlet. It was baseball. Day after day in sunny California he could be found in the vacant lots and ball fields of San Diego.

The Sweetest of Swings

He was first discovered by a Yankee scout, but the Yankees weren't offering enough money in his mother's mind, so they sent him away. Ted then joined the San Diego ball club in the Pacific Coast League. There he was discovered by accident by the great hitter Eddie Collins, who was now the general manager for the Boston Red Sox. Collins was out looking at Bobby Doerr when he saw a hitter taking batting practice. This hitter had the most perfect swing that Collins had ever seen. It was Ted Williams. Collins signed him up immediately.

He joined the Red Sox with quite a cocky attitude and turned off a number of the old-timers. When a teammate said, "Wait till you see Jimmie Foxx hit," Williams responded, "Wait till Foxx sees me hit." But no one could deny that he was right. He called himself Teddy Ballgame and was soon belting high-soaring long balls that impressed everyone. The Red Sox traded away a top hitter to make room for him, and his position on the team was assured.

Ted Williams had one dream when he began playing professional baseball. He hoped that after he retired, he could walk down the street and people would point and say, "There goes Ted Williams, the greatest hitter who ever lived."

In his first year he hit .327, clouted 31 homers, and brought in 145 RBIs, making himself tops in the league. The next year he hit .344. In fact, for 18 out of 19 years, he hit over .300. "Old T.S.W. doesn't have bad years," he once said.

The Natural

Ted was a natural, with the advantages of pure athleticism, a perfect swing, and 20/10 eyesight, which was extraordinarily rare. He could pick up the spin on the ball the instant it left the pitcher's hand. But natural ability was only part of his greatness. He was a perfectionist and never let a detail slip by him. He studied everything, the mechanics of his swing, the pitcher's delivery, the pitcher's history, anything that might give him an edge. He once told the manager that home plate was slightly out-of-line. They checked it. It was.

When he picked out his bats, he would go to Louisville Slugger personally to pick out the wood. They were custom-made 35-ounce bats. And no one was more careful with his bats than he was. He refused to even put them in the cargo area of a plane. He used to yell at his teammates for leaving bats on the grass during night games. He said the moisture could add an ounce. He had long ago decided that bat speed was far more important than bat weight in power hitting, and every extra ounce slowed him down a bit more.

The Last .400 Hitter

His attention to detail paid off. In 1941 Ted Williams couldn't miss. In July of that year his average was as high as .436. The baseball world was watching eagerly. On the morning of the last day of the season, Ted Williams's batting average was an even .400. His manager offered to let him sit out during the two games of the doubleheader. Williams said no. He wanted to say he hit .400 for "the season," and if he sat out, even just for a day, it wouldn't be a full season and he wouldn't deserve it. The first time up, he singled. Then he stroked a home run and two more singles, going 4-for-5 in the first game. He had guaranteed his .400 mark before the second game even began. Adding gravy to that number he went 2-for-3, ending the season with a lofty .406. It hasn't been touched since.

But despite Williams's achievements at the plate, the Red Sox didn't even come close to winning the pennant in 1941. Joe DiMaggio, with his 56-game hitting streak, and the perpetual-winning Yankees took the honors. DiMaggio was voted MVP that year, despite the fact that Williams out hit and outslugged him, leading the league in average and home runs. But Williams could hardly argue with the vote. The streak was impressive.

Unpopular in the Polls

In 1942 Williams won the Triple Crown for the first time. He hit .356, with 36 homers and 137 RBIs. But the MVP award went to another Yankee, second baseman Joe Gordon. In 1947 DiMaggio and Williams, again, were the top MVP vote-getters. This time Williams had won his second Triple Crown, hitting .343, crushing 32 homers, and knocking in 114 RBIs. DiMaggio didn't lead in a single category. But the Yankees had won the pennant again, and DiMaggio copped the MVP award one vote ahead of Williams. Williams must have wondered what he had to do to win.

In 1941, when Williams achieved his tremendous .406 batting average, there was no designation in the score books for sacrifice flies. Even if the fly out scored a run, it was still counted as an at bat. By today's scoring, the 14 sacrifice flies that Williams hit that year would have been 14 less at bats. That would have given him a final season average of .419.

He entered the war, and baseball once again lost a top player in his prime until he returned in 1946. Always one for a show, he smashed a home run in his first at bat, and that year he finally won his first MVP award. He went to his first World Series, but the Red Sox lost to the Cardinals. Williams would never return to the post-season.

He won the MVP award again in 1949, but in 1950 he broke his elbow and was out for the season. The outside world intruded again in 1952 and stole him away from baseball to fight in the Korean War. For the next five years, he played off and on and was at the top of the league in batting average every year.

In 1957 he was back in full form. He won the crown that year with a .388 average and the next year, too, with a .328 average. Midway through the 1960 season, he announced his retirement. And the perfectionist even orchestrated the perfect Hollywood ending. Williams hit one on top of the Boston bullpen roof in the final at bat of his career.

CAREER STATISTICS

Batting average	.344
At bats	7,706
Hits	2,654
Doubles	525
Triples	71
Home runs	521
Runs scored	1,798
Runs batted in	1,839
Walks	2,019

Hack Wilson

Lewis Robert "Hack" Wilson was a standout power hitter for the Chicago Cubs. His biggest mark of fame is his all-time single-season record of 190 RBIs, set in 1930. He also holds the NL record for homers in one season, with 56.

Taking His Hacks

Hack Wilson was born in Elwood City, Pennsylvania, on April 26, 1900. He quit school in the sixth grade to go to work at the locomotive works in nearby Baldwin, Pennsylvania. His many years of swinging heavy hammers gave him the upper-body strength he needed to be a baseball slugger. Even though he stood at only 5'6", he weighed 200 pounds and had tremendous power.

The New York Giants were the ones who first signed Hack in 1923. When he slumped in his third year, they left him unprotected. The Cubs snapped him up and signed him for almost nothing. Then, for the next five years, Hack's home-run total skyrocketed, peaking with 56 in 1930. Every year but his last with the Cubs Wilson batted over .300. He led the league in home runs four times and in RBIs twice.

After 1930, however, Hack Wilson never again put up Hall of Fame numbers. He was a big drinker, and the alcohol proved to be too much for him. It ruined his career. The Cubs traded him to the Cardinals, who traded him to the Dodgers, who, in 1934, finally traded him to the Phillies. He played only seven games for the Phillies, batting a mere .100, and then he retired.

CAREER STATISTICS	
Batting average	.307
At bats	4,760
Hits	1,461
Doubles	266
Triples	67
Home runs	244
Runs scored	884
Runs batted in	1,062
Walks	674

Dave Winfield

David Mark Winfield clouted double-digit home runs in every full year of his career. His total is 465. He knocked in over 100 RBIs eight times in his career and compiled 3,110 hits.

Pick A Sport

Dave Winfield starred in two sports at the University of Minnesota. He was a basketball player and a baseball player. He was so good that he was drafted by four different teams. The San Diego Padres wanted him for baseball. Utah and Atlanta wanted him for basketball. And unbelievably, the Minnesota Vikings wanted him for football, even though he'd never played the sport at college. Winfield went with baseball.

He started off strong. In his first full season with the Padres, he hit 20 home runs. By 1979 his numbers escalated to a .308 average, with 34 home runs and 118 RBIs.

Winfield became a free agent in 1981, and he signed with the Yankees. He played well, individually, but never won a World Championship in New York. Finally, in 1992, playing for the Toronto Blue Jays, Dave won his World Series ring. He notched his 3,000th hit in 1993 with Minnesota and retired with Cleveland in 1995.

CAREER STATISTICS	
Batting average	.283
At bats	11,003
Hits	3,110
Doubles	540
Triples	88
Home runs	465
Runs scored	1,669
Runs batted in	1,833
Walks	1,216

Carl Yastrzemski

Carl Michael "Yaz" Yastrzemski was the last player to win the Triple Crown. When he retired, he was near the top of almost every hitting category. He's in the 3,000 hit club, and has hit 452 home runs in his career. He was inducted into the Hall of Fame in 1989.

Potato Power

Almost from the moment he was born in Southampton, New York, Carl Yastrzemski was a baseball fan, and a Yankee fan at that. His father had wanted to be in the major leagues but hadn't made it, so he was determined that Carl would. The Yastrzemski's owned a potato farm, so the chores that Carl was assigned were chosen specifically to build up his arm and wrist muscles. He worked, and he practiced baseball. And then he was ready for the pros.

Many pro teams wanted him, so he had his pick. And they were all willing to pay unheard of amounts to get this 18-year-old boy who hit .655 in high school. But even though he was a Yankee fan from way back, he didn't get a good feeling at the New York tryouts or in contract discussions. He signed with the Boston Red Sox.

Big Shoes to Fill

It was a good decision. After Yaz played left field for two years in the minors, the position for the Red Sox opened up. But Yaz had a tough job in front of him. The player who had just retired from left field was none other than the incredible Ted Williams. But the Red Sox knew what they were doing when they chose Carl Yastrzemski for the job.

By his second year Yaz was hitting .296, with 19 homers and 94 RBIs. By his third, he'd won the batting crown, also leading the league in hits, doubles, and walks. And in 1967 he won the Triple Crown, with a .326 average, 44 home runs, and 121 RBIs.

That year, 1967, the Red Sox were in an incredibly tight race with the Twins, the Tigers, and the White Sox for the AL pennant. Yaz turned it on. In the last two weeks he hit .522. He drove in 22 runs and belted five home runs. In the final series, he went 7-for-8, and the Red Sox won the pennant on the very last day of the season.

Carl Yastrzemski had a very odd way of batting. He held the bat almost straight up and down, with his hands held high above his head.

Close, but No Cigar

Yaz continued to explode in the World Series, too. He hit .400 and had three homers, but this time it wasn't enough. The Red Sox lost to the St. Louis Cardinals in seven games. Yaz also put up the big numbers, batting .310 in Boston's next World Series in 1975. But once again, the Red Sox lost in seven games. Carl Yastrzemski never won a World Series ring despite his 23 seasons in the majors. He had the misfortune of spending all of those 23 years on the Bambino-cursed Boston Red Sox.

His long career put him second on the all-time list for games played, and third for at bats. With that many years behind him, he almost couldn't help notching over 3,000 hits and over 400 dingers, the first AL player to do it. But as he got older, his skills dropped off a bit. His average never made it above .300 for the last ten years of his career, leaving him with a lifetime average of .285.

CAREER STATISTICS	
Batting average	.285
At bats	11,988
Hits	3,419
Doubles	646
Triples	59
Home runs	4,452
Runs scored	1,816
Runs batted in	1,844
Walks	1,845

Robin Yount

Robin Yount is a member of the 3,000 hit club and thirteenth on the all-time total-hit list with 3,142. He hit 251 home runs in his career, and his lifetime batting average stands at .287.

A Caged Hitter

Robin Yount was born on September 16, 1955 in Danville, Illinois. His family moved to Los Angeles, though, when he was just a baby. Robin's father built him a batting cage when he was in junior high, but he'd destroyed it by the end of the year, hitting baseballs right through it.

Robin was a first-round draft pick by the Brewers in 1973. It took him only a year in the minors before he was made the Brewers' full-time shortstop on Opening Day in 1974.

In 1982 Yount had the best year of his career, hitting .331, leading the league with hits, with 210, and again leading in doubles. He was voted league MVP.

He was voted the MVP again, in 1989, batting .318, with 21 homers. And then in 1992 he reached his biggest milestone. He notched his 3,000th career hit. When asked about his Hall of Fame prospects, Robin Yount just said, "It's not my position to make that decision. I can only say I'm happy with the way my career went."

CAREER STATISTICS

Batting average	.287
At bats	11,008
Hits	3,142
Doubles	583
Triples	126
Home runs	251
Runs scored	1,632
Runs batted in	1,406
Walks	966

Appendix

ALL-TIME HITTING RECORDS

Batting Average

Ty Cobb	.367
Rogers Hornsby	.358
Joe Jackson	.356
Ed Delehanty	.346
Tris Speaker	.345
Billy Hamilton	.345
Ted Williams	.344
Willie Keeler	.343
Dan Brouthers	.342
Babe Ruth	.342

At Bats

Pete Rose	14,053
Hank Aaron	12,364
Carl Yastrzemski	11,988
Ty Cobb	11,429
Eddie Murray	11,336
Robin Yount	11,008
Dave Winfield	11,003
Stan Musial	10,972
Willie Mays	10,881
Brooks Robinson	10,654

Hits

Pete Rose	4,256
Ty Cobb	4,191
Hank Aaron	3,771
Stan Musial	3,650
Tris Speaker	3,514
Carl Yastrzemski	3,419
Honus Wagner	3,418
Eddie Collins	3,313
Willie Mays	3,283
Eddie Murray	3,255

Doubles

Tris Speaker	792
Pete Rose	746
Stan Musial	725
Ty Cobb	724
George Brett	665
Nap Lajoie	658
Carl Yastrzemski	646
Honus Wagner	643
Hank Aaron	624
Paul Waner	603

Single-Season Records

Highest Batting Average—Rogers Hornsby—.424 (1924)
Most At Bats—Willie Wilson—705 (1980)
Most Hits—George Sisler—257 (1920)
Most Doubles—Earl Webb—67 (1931)
Most Triples—Owen Wilson—36 (1912)
Most Home Runs—Roger Maris—61 (1961)
Most Runs Batted In—Hack Wilson—190 (1930)
Most Runs Scored—Billy Hamilton—192 (1894)
Bases on Balls—Babe Ruth—170 (1923)

Triples

Sam Crawford	311
Ty Cobb	297
Honus Wagner	252
Jake Beckley	242
Roger Connor	233
Tris Speaker	223
Fred Clarke	220
Dan Brouthers	205
Joe Kelley	194
Paul Waner	190

Home Runs

Hank Aaron	755
Babe Ruth	714
Willie Mays	660
Frank Robinson	586
Harmon Killebrew	573
Reggie Jackson	563
Mike Schmidt	548
Mickey Mantle	536
Jimmie Foxx	534
Ted Williams	521

Runs Batted In

Hank Aaron	2,297
Babe Ruth	2,211
Lou Gehrig	1,990
Ty Cobb	1,961
Stan Musial	1,951
Jimmie Foxx	1,921
Eddie Murray	1,917
Willie Mays	1,903
Mel Ott	1,861
Carl Yastrzemski	1,844

Runs Scored

Ty Cobb	2,245
Babe Ruth	2,174
Hank Aaron	2,174
Pete Rose	2,165
Willie Mays	2,062
Stan Musial	1,949
Rickey Henderson	1,913
Lou Gehrig	1,888
Tris Speaker	1,882
Mel Ott	1,859

Bases on Balls

Babe Ruth	2,056
Ted Williams	2,019
Joe Morgan	1,865
Carl Yastrzemski	1,845
Rickey Henderson	1,772
Mickey Mantle	1,734
Mel Ott	1,708
Eddie Yost	1,614
Darrell Evans	1,605
Stan Musial	1,599

Index

A

Aaron, Hank, 1–4, 83, 116
  Eddie Mathews and, 95, 96
  Willie Mays and, 99, 101
Abbott, Jim, 83
Alexander, Gary, 115
Alomar, Roberto, 29
Alomar, Sandy, 29, 85
Alvarez, Wilson, 153
Anson, Cap, 5
A-Rod, 136–137
Ashburn, Richie, 152

B

Baerga, Carlos, 29
Bagwell, Jeff, 6–7
Baines, Harold, 153
Baker, Frank, 8, 47
Bambino, 140–143
Banks, Ernie, 9–10, 169–170
Barrow, Ed, 163
Bash Brothers, 25
Bell, Cool Papa, 11
Bell, George, 154
Belle, Albert, 12–13, 161, 162
Bench, Johnny, 14, 169
Berra, Yogi, 15
Bichette, Dante, 83
Big Cat, 110
Big Daddy, 45–46
Big Hurt, 158–159
Big Poison, 166
Black Mike, 36

Boggs, Wade, 16–17

Bonds, Barry, 18–19, 24, 39, 45, 172
Bonds, Bobby, 18–19, 39
Brett, George, 20–21
Brock, Lou, 22
Brodeau, Lou, 137
Bucket Head, 127–128
Bucketfoot Al, 150
Buddha, 127–128

C

Campanella, Roy, 23
Campy, 23
Cannonball, 127–128
Canseco, José, 2, 18, 24–25
Carew, Rod, 26–27, 129, 145
Carter, Joe, 28–29
Cepeda, Orlando, 103
Charlie Hustle, 138–139
Clark, Will, 83, 123, 172
Clemente, Roberto, 30–31
Cobb, Ty, 32–35, 61, 62, 136
  Honus Wagner and, 163, 164
  Nap Lajoie and, 81
  Pete Rose and, 138
  Rogers Hornsby and, 66, 68
  Shoeless Joe and, 70
  Tris Speaker and, 155
Cochrane, Mickey, 36, 47

Cocky Collins, 37
Collins, Eddie, 37, 173–174
Combs, Earle, 38
Comiskey, Charles, 33
Cool Papa, 11
Crime Dog, 105–106

D

Dawson, Andre, 18, 39
Dickey, Bill, 15, 40
DiMaggio, Joe, 41–44, 76, 159
  Mickey Mantle and, 87–88
  Ted Williams and, 175, 176
Doerr, Bobby, 174
Drysdale, Don, 78
Ducky Medwick, 109
Duncan, Mariano, 154

E

Easler, Mike, 162
Edmonds, Jim, 27

F

Fernandez, Tony, 29, 154
Fielder, Cecil, 45–46
Fire Hydrant, 127–128
Foxx, Jimmie, 47–48, 89, 174

G

Gehrig, Lou, 40, 49–52, 103, 158, 170

Cal Ripken and,
130–131
Gehringer, Charlie, 53
Georgia Peach, 32–35
Gibson, Josh, 54
Gonzalez, Juan,
55–56, 168
Gooden, Dwight,
105–106, 148
Gordon, Joe, 176
Gorgeous George, 151
Gray Eagle, 155
Greenberg, Hank, 12,
43, 57
Griffey, Ken, Jr., 56,
58–59, 94, 136
Griffey, Ken, Sr., 58, 59
Guerrero, Pedro, 154
Gwynn, Tony, 45,
60–63

H

Hadley, Bump, 36
Hammerin' Hank, 1–4,
57
Hargrave, Bubbles, 166
Hawk, 39
Henderson, Rickey,
64–65
Hit Dog, 161–162
Hockey Puck, 127–128
Home Run Baker, 8
Hornsby, Rogers,
66–69, 170
Hrbek, Kent, 16

I

Iron Horse, 49–52

J

Jackson, Joe, 70
Jackson, Reggie, 25,
71–72

James, Chris, 29
Johnson, Ban, 35
Johnson, Randy, 108
Johnson, Walter, 33
Joltin' Joe, 41–44
Jones, Chipper, 73–74
Justice, David, 172

K

Kaline, Al, 75, 136
Keeler, Wee Willie, 16,
43, 76
Killebrew, Harmon, 72,
77–78
Killer, 77–78
Kiner, Ralph, 79
Klein, Chuck, 12, 80,
121
Koufax, Sandy, 120

L

Lajoie, Napolean, 34,
81
Langston, Mark, 148
Lansford, Carney, 16
Larkin, Barry, 82–83
Lasorda, Tommy, 123
Little Poison, 165
Lofton, Kenny, 45,
84–85

M

Mad Dog, 86
Madlock, Bill, 86
Man of Steal, 64–65
Mantle, Mickey,
87–90, 91, 152
    Eddie Murray and,
    116
    Willie Mays and,
    99
Maris, Roger, 3, 89,
91–92, 107, 171

Martinez, Edgar,
93–94
Mathews, Eddie,
95–96
Mattingly, Don, 97–98,
106
Mays, Willie, 7, 18,
39, 88, 99–102
    Duke Snider and,
    152
    Eddie Murray and,
    116
McCarthy, Joe, 41, 51
McCovey, Willie,
103–104
McGriff, Fred, 29,
105–106
McGwire, Mark, 2, 25,
83, 107–108, 159
Mechanical Man, 53
Medwick, Joe, 109
Minnesota Squats,
127–128
Mitchell, Kevin, 172
Mize, Johnny, 110
Molitor, Paul, 111–112
Morgan, Joe, 14,
113–114
Mr. Cub, 9–10,
169–170
Mr. October, 71–72
Murderer's Row, 38,
49
Murray, Eddie, 115–116
Murray, Rich, 115
Musial, Stan, 12, 17,
117–118

N

Nettles, Graig, 149

O

Oliva, Tony, 119–120
Ott, Mel, 121